MODERN WORLD NATIONS

China

Second Edition

Gary T. Whiteford and Christopher L. Salter

Series Editor
Charles F. Gritzner
South Dakota State University

CHELSEA HOUSE
PUBLISHERS
An imprint of Infobase Publishing

Frontispiece: Flag of China

Cover: The Pearl River in Shanghai, China

China, Second Edition

Chelsea House
An imprint of Infobase Publishing
132 West 31st Street
New York NY 10001

Library of Congress Cataloging-in-Publication Data

Whiteford, Gary T., 1941–
  China / Gary T. Whiteford and Christopher L. Salter. — 2nd ed.
      p. cm. — (Modern world nations)
  Includes bibliographical references and index.
  ISBN 978-1-60413-621-0 (hardcover)
  1. China—Juvenile literature. I. Salter, Christopher L. II. Title.
  DS706.W58 2010
  951—dc22
                              2009043748

Chelsea House books are available at special discounts when purchased in bulk
quantities for businesses, associations, institutions, or sales promotions. Please call
our Special Sales Department in New York at (212) 967-8800 or (800) 322-8755.

You can find Chelsea House on the World Wide Web at
http://www.chelseahouse.com

Text design by Takeshi Takahashi
Cover design by Alicia Post
Composition by EJB Publishing Services
Cover printed by Bang Printing, Brainerd MN
Book printed and bound by Bang Printing, Brainerd MN
Date printed: April 2010
Printed in the United States of America

10 9 8 7 6 5 4 3 2 1

This book is printed on acid-free paper.

All links and Web addresses were checked and verified to be correct at the time of
publication. Because of the dynamic nature of the Web, some addresses and links
may have changed since publication and may no longer be valid.

Table of Contents

China

Second Edition

1

Introducing China

C hina, which is one of the world's oldest continuous civilizations, has had some form of organized society since before
2000 B.C. The country has made significant contributions
in philosophy, religion, science, math, politics, agriculture, writing,
and the arts. With a population of about 1.35 billion and a land area
of 3.7 million square miles (9.6 million square kilometers), China
is not only a dominant regional power, but also a global one. The
popular image of China is one of large numbers of people using
tremendous energy and effort to transform the land. This process
is dramatically evident in the completion of the world's largest
hydroelectric dam at the Three Gorges narrows of the Chang Jiang
(Yangtze River).

China is a rugged country, with mountains, hills, and plateaus
occupying about 65 percent of the total land area. The highest peak
in the world, Mount Everest, stands on the border between China

and Nepal. Unfortunately for the Chinese people, less than 15 percent of the land is farmable, compared with about 20 percent in the United States. Thus, the people of China, with less than 7 percent of the world's arable land, constantly work to feed 22 percent of the world's population.

China occupies a strategic position in Asia. It is situated on the world's largest landmass, Eurasia, with the largest ocean, the Pacific, as its eastern border. Mainland China extends from 20° north to 53° north latitude, covering 2,300 miles (3,680 km). It stretches from 74° to 134° east longitude. This longitudinal distance of 3,230 miles (5,170 km) means that, when it is noon in the east, it is only early morning in the far western part of the country. China's land boundaries total some 14,000 miles (22,000 km), and China shares national borders with 14 countries. It has an extensive coastline of 9,000 miles (14,500 km), which includes the territorial waters of the Bohai Gulf and three neighboring seas—the Huang Hai (Yellow Sea), the Dong Hai (East China Sea), and the Nan Hai (South China Sea).

The growth of civilization in China has centered on three great river systems, all of which flow from west to east. The northern quarter is drained by the Huang He (Yellow River), which runs approximately 3,000 miles (4,700 km) from the western territory of Tibet to its mouth in Shandong Province. The middle half of the country is drained by the Chang Jiang (Yangtze River), which also originates in Tibet. The Chang Jiang is the longest river in China at 3,900 miles (6,300 km) and has 10 times the water discharge of the Huang He. It is now navigable by ship from Shanghai to the western inland city of Chongqing, more than 900 miles (1,440 km) distant. More than 50 percent of China's population lives in the Chang Jiang basin, because it includes the richer and most productive land in the country and receives adequate rainfall. The southern quarter of China is dominated by the Xi Jiang (West River). It is the shortest of the three major rivers, flowing approximately 1,650 miles (2,655 km) before merging with the Zhu Jiang (Pearl River) in

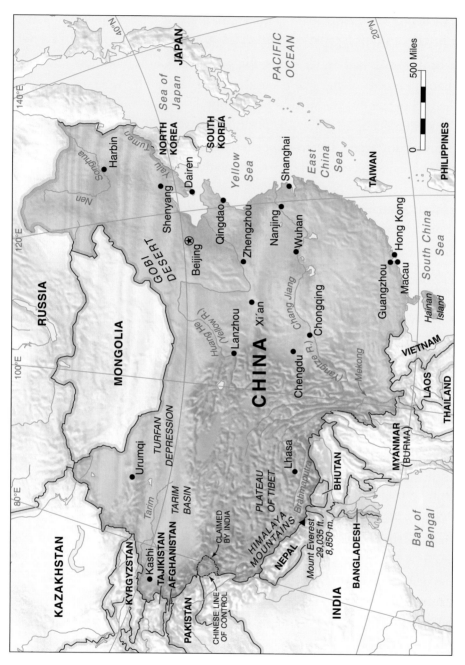

China has an area of 3.7 million square miles (9.6 million square kilometers) and is only slightly smaller than the United States. Located on the Eurasian landmass, China's neighbors include Russia and Mongolia to the north, Afghanistan and Kazakhstan to the west, Nepal and India to the south, and the Pacific Ocean to the east.

the delta. The two vital cities of Guangzhou (formerly Canton) and Hong Kong are situated at the mouth of this river.

These great river systems have been the cheapest and most practical form of transportation in China and were a critical source for irrigation and energy. The river valleys also provided fertile alluvial soils for the surrounding level land. Alluvial soils are stream-deposited material. As a result of these factors, China's population is concentrated along these rivers and reaches its highest and most extensive density near their mouths.

Central to any knowledge of China is an understanding of the location and character of its people. Nine-tenths of the population is of the Han ethnic group, and the remaining one-tenth is divided among 55 other distinct ethnic groups. Traditionally, the Chinese family functioned as a unit and worked the land by plowing, seeding, cultivating, and harvesting. The peasant-agriculturist was the principal bearer of Chinese civilization. Therefore, Chinese history is tied to this continuously productive, agrarian (rural) society. Hundreds of millions of Chinese peasants still work the land. However, one of the most notable changes in the last 25 years has been the increase in the size and number of cities in China, as people move to find work. Large cities help attract foreign investment, and the country plans to expand hundreds of towns into new cities. By 2025, the urban population is expected to make up 55 percent of the total population, up from the current 46 percent.

The Chinese people have long enjoyed strong traditions and values. Confucius (551–479 B.C.), whose teachings and writings have influenced Chinese thought for 2,500 years, was the source of the Confucian Classics. These books functioned as the guide for Chinese civilization, highlighting education and family as the foundation of society. Other philosophies also took hold in China. Taoists believed that people should renounce worldly ambitions and turn to nature and the Tao—the eternal force that permeates everything in nature. Buddhism became a very

As the Chinese economy continues to grow, Chinese citizens are increasingly flocking to urban areas in search of jobs and a higher standard of living. One of China's most populous cities, Shanghai, has 18.8 million residents; by comparison, more than 8.36 million people live in New York City. Above, people cross a busy street in Hong Kong.

powerful belief system for the Chinese. It provided a refuge in the political chaos that followed the fall of the Han Dynasty (206 B.C. to A.D. 220.). By the A.D. 400s, Buddhism was widely embraced throughout China. Over the centuries, openness to new ideas fostered the emergence of many Chinese inventions and discoveries.

The government has always been characterized by some form of central authority, dating as far back as the Xia Dynasty of 2200 B.C. Subsequent dynasties reinforced cultural unity and continuity for the Chinese civilization. One dynasty succeeded another through warfare, with only occasional intrusion by forces outside of China. The relative lack of outside contacts in early centuries allowed China to develop one culture across many regions with a strong sense of national identity. A series of emperors served as political leaders supported by well-equipped armies. The Chinese people believed that their emperors ruled by "A Mandate of Heaven." These dynasties continued over the centuries until the opening of China to the West in the 1800s, with the eventual emergence of the Communist leadership and government in 1949.

China's foreign and economic policies have taken significant twists and turns in the twentieth and twenty-first centuries. This is apparent in the admission of China to the World Trade Organization (WTO) in December 2001 after some 15 years of negotiations. China's entry into the WTO is generally regarded as a most significant event, equal in importance to China's being given a Security Council seat in the United Nations in 1971. Furthermore, China and the Association of Southeast Asian Nations established a free-trade area and a regional trading bloc to begin in 2010, similar to those that exist in Europe and the Americas. From 2004 to 2008, trade volume between China and ASEAN nations doubled from just over $100 billion to more than $200 billion.

China has seen sharp increases in tourism, trade, and foreign investment. Exports comprise 80 percent of China's foreign currency exchange, and light industrial products like small appliances, clothing, and footwear have overtaken agricultural products in economic importance. This growth of China's economic strength translates into increased military strength. Always a concern in such a picture is the claim that mainland China makes for control of the offshore island of Taiwan. As the government of Taiwan continues to ease restrictions on the flow of money to the mainland, tensions may be reduced in this tug-of-war between the small island democracy and the world's most populous marketplace and global factory floor.

This country with the world's largest population also has a wide range of natural resources, from fertile soils to forests to fossil fuels and metals. Its human resources are enormous, and its economic potential seems unlimited. China has a military of some 3 million soldiers, with an additional 1.2 million reserves. It has detonated nuclear bombs. The government has stated that space exploration will become "as essential as electricity." In 2003, China launched its first astronaut (*taikonaut*), and in 2007, it launched its first unmanned lunar orbiter as part of its space program.

It is important to learn as much about China as possible and to better understand and appreciate its character from every possible angle. It is a country whose history is unique and defies the Western mind. In the coming decades, China is very likely to continue in its role as one of the dominant world powers. It is vital, therefore, in today's interrelated world, to know all that one can about this remarkable country.

2

Physical
Landscapes

There are many ways to look at China's landscape. It is important
to remember, however, that the natural and human landscapes
have been continually changing over the centuries. Well-known
geographer G.B. Cressey once remarked that the most significant ele-
ment in the Chinese landscape is not the soil, vegetation, or climate,
but the people. In this very old land, one can scarcely find a place
untouched by humans. Large parts of China's south and north are now
stripped of trees by human activity. Over a span of 80 centuries, Chinese culture and settlement have expanded from the original core area
in the middle Huang He to the nation's present-day borders.

China's natural landscapes have greatly affected its historical
development. Mountains comprise nearly one-third of China's area,
and such rugged terrain has hindered cultural and ethnic blending for centuries. Besides the numerous high mountains, extensive

plateaus, rolling hills, inhospitable deserts, enclosed inland basins, and extensive fertile low plains are found in China. Such variety allowed the Chinese people to use the land in many different ways.

One fundamental way to understand China's natural landscapes is to divide the country into two regions—China Proper (Inner China) and Frontier China (Outer China—Xijang, Qinghai, Xinjiang, Nei Mongol, Ningxia). The boundary marks a contrast between a settled, frequently irrigated, and intensely farmed area and a marginal dry-farming area supplemented with agricultural enclaves, like the oases of the northwestern deserts. One is a region of huge cities and settled villages based on intensive agriculture, while the other is an area that features animals grazing on the plateaus. It is in Frontier China that people like the Mongols, Kazaks, Tibetans, Uighurs, Manchus, and other minority groups live. In contrast, overwhelming numbers of Han Chinese live in China Proper. Just as sophisticated rice culture helped shape the agricultural scene of the southeast and the east, so the care of sheep, goats, camels, horses, and cattle helped shape the nomadic lifestyles in the north and the west. These peoples were not tied to the land, as their eastern counterparts were. The two regions are roughly comparable in size, but less than 5 percent of the population lives in Frontier China. Two-thirds of China is only sparsely populated, making the density of settled places even more pronounced.

CHINA PROPER

China Proper (eastern China), a region of hills and plains, encompasses the cultural, agricultural, population, and industrial core of the country. It is a gentle land of alluvial plains, fertile river valleys, and rolling hills. It is this part of the country that has been worn down by centuries of human occupancy and activity. From the complex network of water channels in this area, shipping routes were established that fostered coastal development. China Proper contains four distinct landscape regions: the northeast, the north-central, the south, and the southwest.

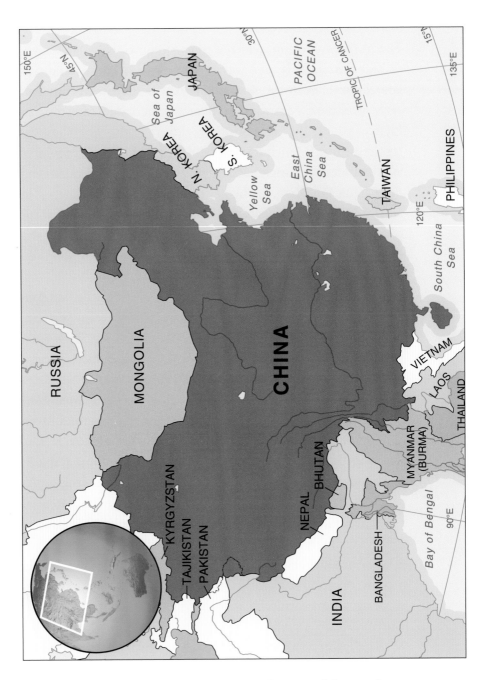

With several mountain ranges, an expansive desert, and thousands of rivers, China is one of the most geographically diverse countries in the world. Because each region has its own unique terrain, individual provinces may have their own cultures and customs that are vastly different from those of another area.

NORTHEAST REGION

The northeast region, referred to as Dongbei, is better known as Manchuria. This area was home to the Manchus and was later dominated by Russia and Japan in the nineteenth and early twentieth centuries. It features the large Manchurian Plain, a productive agricultural region that also holds important resources. Manchuria contains three of China's provinces and includes the Xingan Mountains to the west and north and the Chang Bai Shan to the southeast, along the border with North Korea. These are important timber-producing areas, with oak and other hardwoods. Not fully developed until the early twentieth century, the region now accounts for about 20 percent of China's farmland.

The climate of the northeast region allows only one crop to be produced per year. During the spring, wheat, corn, sorghum, millet, soybeans, and sugar beets are the chief crops. Low temperatures, thin soils, frost, spring drought, and summer–autumn floods are the main natural hazards facing this region.

The Amur River forms part of the northern Manchurian boundary with Russia. Its largest tributary, the Songhua River, along with lesser tributaries, form one of the great river networks in the country. It is second only to the Chang Jiang in annual discharge. As a result, irrigation is not lacking when required, and the surrounding rugged landscape has potential for hydroelectric power. The Second Songhua River is famous for its Fengman hydroelectric facility, along with its huge reservoir, Songhua Lake—just south of Jilin. River boundaries are a common feature of this region. The Yalu and Tumen rivers separate China from its increasingly problematic neighbor, North Korea.

The lower Liao River marks the southern part of Northeast China. It empties into the Bohai Gulf near the Liaodong Peninsula. This area has a more temperate climate and can sustain three crops over a two-year period. It is an important place for the production of fruit, fish, and a variety of silk.

The area is experiencing dramatic environmental problems, such as soil erosion caused by deforestation due to the growth of steel and industrial production centered in Shenyang and Anshan.

The northeast has undergone numerous periods of promise and despair. Japanese occupation between 1931 and 1945 was aggressively exploitative. Later, from 1950 to 1970, the Communists made the development of resources in the northeast a priority. In part, this growth was tied to the region's considerable mineral wealth. Iron ore deposits and coalfields are concentrated in the Liao Basin. Other plentiful metals include aluminum ore, lead, and zinc. The area also has relatively extensive oil reserves. Plentiful resources make the northeast the second-largest iron and steel center in China. Harbin is the main commercial center because of its strategic position, where five rail lines converge.

NORTH-CENTRAL REGION

North-Central China is dominated by the North China Plain, which fronts the Bohai Gulf and the Yellow Sea. The physical landscape almost lacks elevation and is dominated by two major river valleys. The Huang He (Yellow River) and the Chang Jiang (Yangtze River) to the south are the main lifelines of the region. Historically, this area has been the center of Chinese civilization. Today, it remains one of the world's most heavily populated agricultural areas. The region has been the cultural, political, and economic center of China for thousands of years, and six ancient capitals of China are located here.

As the cradle of Chinese agriculture, the Loess Plateau is important in this region. For over 60 centuries, hundreds of millions of peasants have lived on and cultivated this land. However, misuse, overuse, and overgrazing have led to very destructive soil erosion, some of the worst in the world. Nowhere else in China has the struggle by the people to overcome nature been more apparent.

Loess is a fine, wind-borne yellow-grained dust with a top layer that forms an easily cultivated soil. It comes primarily from the winds that scour the Gobi Desert. Millions of cave dwellings have been excavated from loess because it is able to stand in vertical cliffs. These dwellings were warm in winter and cool in summer. The landscape can change constantly as loess is picked up as silt by rivers. The abundance of this yellow soil in the waters of the Huang He gives it its name, the Yellow River. As the river descends from the Loess Plateau to the broad eastern plain, its gradient is very low, and spring flooding often occurs. The river is referred to as "China's Sorrow," because of these floods over the centuries. Yet, the silt deposits brought by the flooding have made the North China Plain a rich agricultural area.

Dikes and dams have always been part of the river systems in this part of China. Records show seven catastrophic shifts of the Huang He river channel and another 26 large-scale shifts, from 600 B.C. to 1950. One breach in 1938 left 900,000 people dead and 13 million more homeless. Major floods can force one million people to work at moving earth and sandbags to try to hold back the waters. Because of the levees (natural and man-made dikes) and the continual buildup of silt, the riverbed in some places is higher than the surrounding plain. This makes the flooding problem worse, because once a levee breaks and causes a flood, the runoff water has no place to re-enter the river.

In this part of China, the people have used water and rivers skillfully over the centuries. Rivers were the original highways for transporting people and goods, and they continue to play a major role today. Inland waterways have long been important. Canals were dug as early as 500 B.C. The famous Grand Canal, at a length of 1,114 miles (1,770 km) was built from Beijing to Hangzhou. Construction on the canal began in 600 B.C. and was not fully completed until 1,200 years later. It is the longest canal in the world and has served as a major water and com-mercial link for the movement of goods and people between southern and northern China.

SOUTH REGION

The Qin Ling Mountains, north of the Chang Jiang, form a significant geographic line in the South Region. These mountains separate the dry, northern wheat-growing areas from the warm, humid, southern rice-growing areas. The northern slopes of the Qin Ling are short and steep, and the foothills are marked sharply by a great fault line. The southern slopes are rather long and gentle. Almost half of the land is original forest, where the giant panda and the golden-haired monkey still survive.

South of the Qin Ling Mountains lies the Sichuan Basin (220,000 sq. mi, or 569,800 sq. km), which contains the Chang Jiang. It is one of the largest inland basins in the country, occupying nearly 50 percent of Sichuan Province. The red sandstone soil mixed with purple shale give the basin its common "Red Basin" name. Surrounded by mountains, the basin enjoys a milder winter than parts of the middle and lower Chang Jiang plains. Relative humidity can be high during the year, and parts of the basin can experience foggy days. The Sichuan Basin has been famous for centuries as an attractive and productive land. It has been intensively cultivated for more than 2,000 years and has one of the world's highest concentrations of rice paddies.

The nearby Chengdu Plain has long been the base for commercial grain and rapeseed (canola) oil in Sichuan Province. The triple-cropping system (two crops of rice, followed by one crop of rapeseed or wheat) predominates. Irrigation greatly supports agriculture, and the famous Du Jiang irrigation system built in 250 B.C. has been operating uninterrupted with only improvements and expansion.

Within the basin are the magnificent Wushan Mountains and the spectacular Three Gorges. Here, the Chang Jiang, or "Long River," is forced to flow through a narrow 150-mile-long (240 km), steep-walled valley no greater than 350 feet (107 meters) wide—slightly more than the length of a football field. The Sanxia, or Three Gorges Dam, has been constructed to alleviate downstream flooding, produce inexpensive

The Three Gorges Dam highlights one of the major challenges in modern China: providing for a growing population with limited resources. Completed in 2006, the Three Gorges Dam is 7,660 feet (2,335 meters) long and 607 feet (185 meters) high and is the largest dam in the world. Above, an upstream view of the Three Gorges region.

hydroelectricity, and improve upstream navigation. With the dam's ship-lock system, 10,000-ton freighters have been able to reach Chongqing six months a year, making this city of some six million (with 30 million in its municipal region) the world's largest inland port.

As the Chang Jiang leaves the restricted confines of the Three Gorges, it meanders sluggishly across the flat terrain of its middle and lower course. Numerous low mountains and hills encircle this middle plain. The lakes here have acted as flood reservoirs for the Chang Jiang during the high-water summer monsoon season. (Monsoons are seasonal winds that are wet in summer and dry in winter.) The lower plain of the river lies less than 10 feet (3 m) above sea level, and this wetland environment has a patchwork of rice paddies and fish farms. These are linked by an extensive network of streams and canals. The force of the water flow of the Chang Jiang is 17 times greater than that of the Huang He. The Chang Jiang is the third-longest river in the world, only 200 miles (322 km) shorter than the Nile, the longest.

Cities located along the river here are often referred to as the "ovens of China," as they experience high summer humidity. The lower part of the Chang Jiang lacks the protection of nearby mountains and thus can have colder winters, light snow, and periodic heavy fog. This part of China is influenced by a humid, subtropical climate. When high temperatures and heavy rainfall come together, the opportunity exists for the intensive triple-cropping system of two crops of rice, followed by one crop of wheat or barley. Frost damage, however, can be a problem owing to the east coast location.

The delta of the Chang Jiang is one of the oldest cultivated and irrigated areas in all of China. Competing for land is the city of Shanghai, with an exploding population of 18.8 million and an expanding industrial complex. The area is an example of how urban development is causing prime rural land to disappear.

In the extreme southeast lies another productive area in the delta of the Pearl River and Xi Jiang (West River), near Hong Kong. This region has ample water and favorable high temperatures. The river plains in the south can support triple cropping with rice, sugarcane, and sweet potatoes. Terraced and alluvial rice-paddy fields and large fish farms also coexist here.

Hong Kong, a city of 7 million people, with a huge commercial and shipping center, and nearby Macau, with a half-million people, compete for land in this delta region. Urban expansion and pollution are constant problems. The surrounding low mountains have suffered much from deforestation and soil erosion.

SOUTHWEST REGION

The Yunnan-Guizhou Plateau of the southwest is situated between southeast China and the Tibetan Plateau. It is China's most physically stunning region, dotted with high ridges and deep gorges. Elevations range from 3,000 to 7,000 feet (914 to 2,134 m). The region is quite wet because of the Indian and Pacific monsoons. The border areas with Southeast Asia are underdeveloped and have an extensive rain forest.

Part of the stunning landscape was created by water erosion on thousands of square miles of limestone rock, or karst, in the Guilin region. The nearby Li River wanders through haystack-shaped hills that stand 1,200 feet (366 m) or more above the surrounding lowlands. These spectacular hills are found in few other places in the world.

FRONTIER CHINA

Frontier China has gorgeous but quite inhospitable scenery. It includes the world's highest mountain, Mount Everest, which stands 29,035 feet (8,850 m) above sea level, and the world's second-lowest place of dry land, the Turfan Depression, which is 505 feet (154 m) below sea level. Frontier China also contains the world's most barren deserts, the Gobi and the Taklamakan. Huge swamps, such as those of the Qaidam Basin, are found in the northern part of the Tibetan Plateau, with virgin forests and extensive grass-covered steppes scattered throughout. Much of Frontier China is an inland drainage area, which is a pattern of streams or rivers that drain toward the center of a basin instead of toward the sea. For this reason, Frontier China was cut off from the extensive system of inland waterways that developed throughout the east of the country.

Frontier China and China Proper were effectively joined together politically under the Manchu (or Qing) Dynasty, mostly during the eighteenth century. This process created what is now recognized as the nation of China. During the last two centuries, Han Chinese migrants have actively extended their influence into Frontier China.

The one great route that joined China Proper to Frontier China was the famous Chinese trade route, the Silk Road. Trade on this 4,000-mile (6,437 km) route began around 140 B.C. It eventually linked the Chinese and Roman empires with trade focused on Chinese silks, jade, pottery, fruits, and paintings. From Rome came gold, glassware, wool, and linen fabrics. And going both directions were ideas, religions, and the general spread of knowledge. The Silk Road looped north and south of the scorching Taklamakan Desert and rose high through the mountain passes across the Pamirs. The Himalayas in the southwestern part of the country effectively seal off China from India, Nepal, and Bhutan. In the shadow of these mountains to the north lies the massive Tibetan Plateau. The 965,000-square-mile plateau (2.5 million sq km) has an average height of 14,765 feet (4,500 m) above sea level. It accounts for one-fourth of the Chinese landmass but contains less than one percent of China's population. Also included in this region are other great mountain ranges: the Karakorum Shan (*shan* means "mountains"), separating China from India and Pakistan; and the Kunlun Shan, separating the plateau from the Xinjiang Autonomous Region to the north and west.

Some of the great rivers of Asia have their source in the Tibetan Plateau. The Huang He (Yellow) and Chang Jiang (Yangtze) flow into China Proper. The Mekong, Irrawaddy, Brahmaputra, and Salween rivers also have their source on the plateau.

North of the Kunlun Shan lies the oval-shaped Qaidam Basin—a transitional area between the frigid Tibetan Plateau and the arid northwest. The basin is a rich salt-mining region, and nearly all of China's potassium reserves are found here. The basin is also believed to have extensive petroleum reserves.

To the far northwest of the Tibetan Plateau are the Xinjiang-Mongolian Uplands, another environmentally inhospitable region. Two great mountain ranges, the Tien Shan and the Altai Mountains, intrude into this region and encompass several large depressions or basins—the Tarim Basin, the Turfan Depression, and the Jungar Basin.

The Tarim Basin contains the only warm temperate desert in China. Several crops may be grown where water is available. The basin runs more than 1,000 miles (1,609 km) west-east and about 400 miles (644 km) north-south. Within this basin lies the barren Taklamakan Desert, which measures 127,414 square miles (330,000 sq km) in area. The Taklamakan is the largest sand desert in China and the second largest in the world. The name of this so-called "sea of death" translates as "go in, not come out." This area is believed to have great potential for oil deposits, and there is evidence of natural gas and several minerals. On a huge salty marshland, just east of the Taklamakan, is Lop Nor, the site where China's 32 underground nuclear bomb tests were conducted from 1964 to 1988.

The Turfan Depression was the site of an ancient underground irrigation system, called a karez, developed between the eighth and tenth centuries. The karez—also used in other parts of Southwest Asia—transformed the area into a garden of grapes, melons, and palm trees.

The Xinjiang Autonomous Region has large open basins surrounded by mountains and can become very hot in the summer. It is so far inland that there is hardly any rainfall, and settlement is confined to the foothills and oases that surround the depressions. At 617,760 square miles (1.6 million sq km), it is the largest province in China. Yet only 20 million people live there.

The Altai Mountains lie north of the Xinjiang-Mongolian Uplands. They stretch northwest to southeast more than 1,240 miles (2,000 km) along the Sino-Russian-Mongolian border.

Only the middle section lies within Chinese territory. The southeastern edge eventually merges into the vast level expanse known as the Gobi Desert. These mountains are the source for rivers that flow into the Jungar Basin.

Part of the Gobi Desert lies in the independent nation of Mongolia, but most of it extends into China's Inner Mongolia. The Gobi is the world's highest desert in elevation and northernmost in latitude. As a result, it is one of the coldest of all deserts. This area, with its interior continental location, is isolated from strong winds and moisture-laden storms. There is enough wind, however, to bring some moisture to support low shrubs and grasses and to promote extensive livestock raising.

To the south of the Gobi Desert is the Ordos Plateau and Desert. The region is easily defined. The Great Wall is to the south and the other three sides form the loop of the Huang He as it flows north, east, and then south. Access to water allows for irrigation and fertile soils. This is one of China's most threatened areas. It is vulnerable to environmental change and desertification—the spread of desert conditions and desert lands into semiarid, or short grasslands, or even woodland areas, as a result of human settlement and activity. Major causes are overgrazing, woodland cutting, and farming in areas of uncertain precipitation. Desertification has become a major problem for China, as the desert has migrated eastward to within 50 miles (80 km) of Beijing, the nation's capital. Occasionally, sandstorms can even close down the Beijing airport. Since the 1980s the loss of prime farmland has been considerable as the large urban centers along the Chang Jiang and east coast have rapidly expanded their industrial and residential development. From 1996 to 2004, China's annual loss of farmland exceeded one million hectares (about 3,900 square miles). Such losses have come from government development, but also, increasingly, from informal and illegal land transfers to developers. Golf courses and housing tracts are replacing paddy land all along the margins of growing Chinese cities.

CLIMATE

China falls within five major climatic zones. These range from cold temperate to subtropical and tropical. The country also experiences climatic extremes. More than 30 percent of China is almost completely arid, but in other parts of the country, tropical rain forests exist. The weather patterns are highly seasonal, largely influenced by the annual monsoon cycle that impacts the southeastern coast.

The mountain topography modifies the weather systems to produce very different regional conditions. The biggest problem in the north and west is the lack of rainfall. Large areas receive less than 5 inches (12.5 centimeters) per year, and agriculture, if possible at all, relies heavily on irrigation. East China receives enough rainfall for farming, but the Qin Ling Mountain range marks a geographic line. South of the range, there is a surplus of water and double and triple cropping is possible. North of this range, there is insufficient water and heavy reliance on irrigation from rivers. Monsoon rains can be unreliable, so rainfall varies from year to year. Droughts and floods are always a part of China's climatic picture and a challenge for its people. The management of water resources has been a major concern for farmer and government alike.

Typhoons can be a source of moisture from July to October. They develop in the Pacific and strike the southern and eastern coasts, impacting China more than any other country in the world. An average of seven typhoons strike the country each year. They can move inland some 300 miles (483 km) and last several days, releasing great quantities of water. Typhoons bring winds that have been known to reach 200 miles (322 km) per hour, causing severe damage and coastal flooding. Most weaken within several hours of landfall, however.

Regional temperature varies more in winter than in summer. The northeast and west regions and interior locations have low average winter temperatures, in the 22°F (−5.6°C) range. North of the Qin Ling Mountains, the winter temperatures also are below freezing. Beijing can average 23°F (-5°C) in January, while Guangzhou near Hong Kong in the south averages 59°F (15°C). Because of the mountain elevation and inland location, winters in western parts of China are below average in temperature for their latitude. Summers are excessively hot and humid, except on the Tibetan Plateau.

EARTHQUAKES AND VOLCANOES

China has kept records of destructive earthquakes almost as long as history has been written. Earth's surface is composed of 12 giant rock plates that average 70 miles (113 km) in thickness. These crustal plates are in motion and push against each other, triggering earthquakes. China sits on the Eurasian major tectonic plate, which borders three other major tectonic plates in the region. The northward-moving Indian-Australian plate collides with China in the Himalayan region, pushing the mountains upward. Just east of China, the Eurasian plate intersects two other major plates near Japan. This is part of the Pacific Ring of Fire, a circle of earthquake and volcanic zones that surrounds the Pacific Ocean.

The Chinese have always been interested in earthquakes, and in A.D. 132, they devised the first seismograph to measure and record vibrations in the earth. In 1556, Shaanxi Province experienced a devastating earthquake (believed to be higher than eight on the Richter scale), which killed more than one million people. Similar large-magnitude earthquakes have struck the region over the centuries. Chinese scientists have compiled a 3,000-year catalog of earthquakes, and 500 destructive ones have occurred during the last 1,000 years. One of every 16 earthquakes that hit China reaches a magnitude 8 or greater on the Richter scale. Since 1900, 48 deadly earthquakes have killed a total of more than one million people in China. In 1976, Tangshan, an industrial city 85 miles (137 km) east of Beijing, lost some 650,000 people in an 8.2-magnitude earthquake. In May 2008, an earthquake in Sichuan killed 80,000 people and led to major protests about the weak construction apparent in the region's public schools. The lack of earthquake-proof buildings throughout the country has made the Chinese people vulnerable when earthquakes strike.

PROBLEMS FOR THE LAND

Centuries of agriculture have dramatically modified China's plant and animal life. It is thought that much of China was once heavily forested. Deciduous trees in the south gave way to coniferous trees in the north. Pockets of tropical rain forest are still found in the south from the interior Yunnan-Assam, India, border to offshore Hainan Island. Generally, grassland, steppe, and desert dominate the north and northwest, and the woodlands are confined to the central and southeastern parts of the country. The Tibetan Plateau has the extensive meadows and alpine vegetation common in high-altitude locations.

The extent of deforestation over the last 50 years has had massive consequences for the country. A United Nations report calculated that more than one-third of China's healthy forests located near high-density populations are under intense pressure. Another 55 percent of China's forest area is threatened as economic growth results in an increasing demand for wood. The country is the second-largest importer of timber in the world. Because of desertification that is particularly noticeable in the north and west, the government tried to return 17 percent of the country to forest cover by 2000. Tree planting focused on the upper reaches of major river systems such as the Chang Jiang, Huang He, and Liao to stabilize the land and provide needed timber. A large project involves planting trees along a protective green belt stretching 4,350 miles (7,000 km) from the northeast to Xinjiang in the far west. This is known as China's Great Green Wall. Such projects require irrigation and steady care—which are difficult to guarantee in sparsely settled, arid environments.

A 2008 earthquake in Sichuan Province devastated the region and destroyed buildings, many of which were local schools and dormitories housing students. Despite recent reforms requiring new structures to be able to withstand major quakes, many buildings were damaged and others collapsed, leading to the deaths of thousands.

WILDLIFE

Even with intensive human occupancy, enough wilderness still exists in some areas to support varied wildlife—like reptiles, elephants, tigers, monkeys, and the famous giant panda. Some notable surviving Chinese wildlife includes the great paddle-fish of the Yangtze, the small species of alligator in east-central China, and the giant salamander in western China. Diversity of animal life is greatest in the ranges and valleys of the Tibetan border. The giant panda is found most often near the Sichuan Province–Tibet border. The future for this animal, however, remains bleak, because it has a particular habitat and must consume about 45 pounds (20 kilograms) of a specific type of bamboo daily.

The World Resources Institute identified some frightening declines in China's biodiversity. Some 30,000 plants, 1,100 birds, 394 land mammals, 340 reptiles, and 263 amphibians are known to be threatened. Today, about 8 percent of China's land area is set aside as nature reserves.

Locusts are perhaps China's most destructive species. For centuries, more than 60 types of locusts have caused major agricultural damage. The East Asian flying locust is a particular menace. The North China Plain has been hardest hit over the centuries, as locust invasions have been linked to droughts, floods, and famines.

COASTAL FEATURES

The Chinese coastline—more than 9,000 miles (14,500 km)—has made the country both a continental and a maritime nation. Off China's coast are some 5,000 rocky islands, the largest being Hainan and Taiwan. These islands have created a zone of inland seas that provided sheltered routes for early trade between China and the islands of the East Indies. Along the coast, China felt the greatest political pressures exerted by Western Europe in the form of "treaty ports" established during the nineteenth century. Treaty ports were cities opened to foreign trade. These treaty ports, most notably in Shanghai, were privileged enclaves. Foreigners who lived there came under the jurisdiction of their home country's law rather than China's—leading to intense anger among the Chinese.

China's overseas relations with the world were much less important historically than contacts made along its land frontiers. However, near the end of the first millennium A.D., improvements were made in Chinese shipbuilding. A powerful navy developed briefly during the 1400s in the Ming Dynasty, but inland defense was the priority.

Generally, the coast borders a broad continental shelf with water depths from 98 feet to more than 328 feet (30 m to more than 100 m). The central sea basin of the South China Sea is deeper in places. The extensive area between the Yellow Sea and the East China Sea contains a broad and rich petroleum-bearing region that is 300 nautical miles (556 km) wide.

The Chang Jiang and Pearl River deltas were developed for irrigation and fish farming. Besides the intricate fish farming, offshore and deep-sea fishing yield about 17 million tons a year, a very dramatic increase since the 1950s. The Chinese fishery is one of the largest in the world, accounting for 15 percent of the total global catch. The variety of fish and shellfish is vast. Lobster, crab, mackerel, herring, eel, shark, sardine, and sturgeon are just some of the choices. Still, fisheries are a weak part of China's economy.

China has established 15 major seaports. Since the late 1970s, the country has given greater attention to the coastal cities, creating a number of "special economic zones." These zones are manufacturing areas that use tax, tariff, special political accommodations, and investment benefits to attract foreign investors.

This is only an overview of China's natural landscapes. It is vital to realize that the landscape is of fundamental importance, not only to the past but also for the future. It is essential to know the character and composition of this land area to better understand and appreciate how and why the Chinese people interact with their surroundings.

3

China Through the Centuries

C hinese civilization is ancient. The country had dynastic rule for most of its recorded history. A succession of emperors, or rulers in the same line of descent, governed the country. These rulers established the basic pattern of imperial bureaucratic government that lasted until the twentieth century. Usually, dynasties changed through conflicts and battles, and capital cities often moved as well. Among the major dynasties were the Qin (221–206 B.C.), the Han (206 B.C.–A.D. 220), Tang (A.D. 618–907), Song (A.D. 960–1279), Mongol or Yuan (A.D. 1279–1368), Ming (A.D. 1368–1644), and Qing (A.D. 1644–1911).

China has the longest continuous history of any civilization in the world, but the exact origins of the Chinese people and their culture are unknown. Early humans are known to have lived in China more than a half-million years ago. In 1929, the discovery of Peking

Man in a cave southwest of Beijing (formerly Peking) on the North China Plain shows that people lived there from perhaps 700,000 years ago until around 200,000 years ago. Archaeological finds elsewhere in China suggest several similar cultures at the same time. It is likely that the Huang He Valley, like the river valleys of Egypt and Mesopotamia, supported settlement from very early times. It appears that several ethnic groups and centers of early culture gradually mixed to produce the civilization that has continued over the centuries.

Starting at 7000 B.C., agriculture began to develop in several areas in China. Early farming centers may have included the Middle Huang He (Yellow River) and its western tributary, the Wei valley; the lower Chang Jiang (Yangtze River) Valley; and adjacent coastal plains of the southeast. Discoveries have revealed the existence of a Neolithic culture at numerous sites in China. The Neolithic period dates from the latter part of the fourth millennium B.C. until the onset of the Bronze Age (2100–1400 B.C.). This era was characterized by finely fashioned flint and stone, with the beginning of crop cultivation, animal domestication, and pottery making.

EARLY SETTLEMENT

Chinese legends mention gods and demigods in what are now Gansu and Shaanxi provinces of North China. From the legendary first man, Pan Gu, came a series of rulers, and finally, the emergence of the Yellow Emperor around 2550 B.C. This emperor is said to have expanded the boundaries of the empire. From 2300 to 2140 B.C., the famous rulers Yao, Shun, and Yu are mentioned. These are the first monarchs identified in the Shu Ching classics and were later regarded as model rulers by Confucius. Dates and details are uncertain, but Yu the Great is said to have solved flood problems and to have founded the first dynasty, the Xià (or Hsia), which possibly dated from 2205 to 1765 B.C. Although its existence remains in question, many Chinese scholars accept the Xià as a historical reign. At this time, the system of hereditary kingship was created, evolving into the centralized imperial system that lasted for several thousand years.

About 2100 B.C., the Chinese Bronze Age began and brought significant development. This was the age when bronze, made of copper and tin, was used to create objects. Later alloys were added, and then iron, a much harder metal, replaced bronze. At that time, Tang the Accomplished overthrew a tyrant king and founded another dynasty, the Shang or Yin Dynasty, which lasted from 1600 to 1050 B.C. Exact dates are unknown, but the existence of this dynasty has been confirmed.

There appears to be evidence to link parts of southeast China—the present-day provinces of Guangxi, Guangdong, and Fujian—to settlement areas farther south in the area of Vietnam. Influences from Southeast Asia came to China during the Neolithic period and were important for many centuries.

Early rice cultivation formed the basis for settlement along the Chang Jiang and Huai River valleys. Excavations show that this occurred about 10,000 years ago. Rice cultivation spread down the river valleys and along the East China coast. Domestication of dogs, pigs, and water buffalo became an integral part of settlements. Pottery artifacts also pointed to a progressively refined culture, as did evidence of a writing system and wheeled chariots.

At this time, during the Shang Dynasty, the idea of the Chinese state was forming. The Shang kings controlled most of the Huang He plain, including Shandong, Hebei, and Henan provinces, and parts of the provinces of Shaanxi and Shanxi to the immediate west. Archaeological evidence indicates that the Shang state went well beyond these borders. The Shang period was marked by the sophisticated use of bronze and pottery molds. This culture was quite different from other civilizations of that time.

Confucius, one of the most revered figures in Chinese history, was a teacher, philosopher, and political theorist. His three major teachings—the importance of rituals, education, and family—have become ingrained in Chinese culture and traditions. Above, a statue of Confucius at a temple.

FEUDAL STATES

From 1100 to 221 B.C., a rival tribal group emerged to challenge the Shang Dynasty. The Zhou people, located in present-day Shaanxi Province, extended their power to the Huang He Valley and overthrew the Shang by force. A feudal system was put in place and became highly organized. The territory was divided into small states, governed by Zhou clansmen and supporters.

Zhou power lasted more than 800 years, longer than any other Chinese dynasty. Its decline came at the same time that people and animals migrated on the steppes in northern China. Around 900 B.C., armies were more mobile, with armed horse riders. Feudal states evolved to have independent armies competing with each other in incessant wars. The Zhou Dynasty, though depleted of its power, existed for another 500 years, from 771 to 221 B.C. Historical records mark the earlier years as the Spring and Autumn period and the latter part as the Warring States period. It was a time of cultural advances in philosophy, the arts, and technology and a prelude to the first great imperial age in China.

The principal states of northern China were collectively known as Zhongguo, the "Middle Kingdoms." The Chinese considered their culture the center of the universe, and they felt they were surrounded by barbaric people outside their territory and isolated from other sophisticated cultures of India and western Eurasia.

This period saw the development of great social and political philosophical thought in China. Confucius, who lived from 551 to 479 B.C., introduced systematic philosophy and ethics to the problems of government and the people. Mencius, his disciple, stressed the ideas of moral principles. Other philosophers with many different ideas emerged and influenced existing rulers. Taoism, another school of philosophy, also appeared. It was a more contemplative approach, compared with the rigid principles of Confucianism.

FIRST EMPEROR OF THE QIN DYNASTY

By 221 B.C., King Zheng of Qin completed the conquest of all the Chinese states. He declared himself the first emperor of the Qin Dynasty. As the dynasty evolved, it expanded and consolidated its territory by following the guidance of ministers versed in legal philosophy. This approach helped the dynasty avoid direct battle. An area approximately equal to that of China Proper was unified under one ruler.

The 15-year Qin Dynasty brought together a diverse cultural and linguistic territory. It was successful in centralizing authority and standardizing currency, transportation routes, weights, measures, and written script. The empire's main problems were threats from outside the northern frontier. The Chinese often protected towns and cities with large walls. Longer walls were also built, extending along the northern edge of the Chinese cultural center located to the south. Different construction materials (based on local conditions) were used—compressed earth or stone and brick. Eventually, the first Great Wall was completed in 214 B.C., through forced labor and with great loss of life. Much of the Great Wall seen now was built during the Ming Dynasty. Today, the Great Wall stretches some 4,500 miles (7,250 km), equal to the distance from New York City to Las Vegas and back.

The burial ground for the Qin emperor, discovered in 1974 by local farmers, is quite elaborate and unique. Subsequent archaeological digs revealed a mausoleum containing the now-famous Terracotta Warriors. These 8,000 life-size statues of soldiers stand in military formation. Some people refer to the figures as the Eighth Wonder of the World. The burial ground is near Xian in Shaanxi Province.

HAN DYNASTY

The Qin Dynasty fell quickly. It marked the first time in Chinese history that a peasant uprising toppled a dynasty. A military officer who was a commoner declared himself emperor and

Built over the span of three centuries, the Great Wall of China connected other walls to create one long structure to protect various kingdoms from invaders. The Great Wall is about 4,500 miles (7,300 km) long and runs westward from Bo Hai, a gulf on China's east coast, into Central Asia.

created the Han Dynasty, which lasted more than 400 years from 206 B.C. to A.D. 220. Han China rivaled the Roman Empire in achievements and power. Technological advances included gunpowder, paper, porcelain, and the wheelbarrow. The teachings of Confucius became the cornerstone of state thought, and the people accepted the absolute power of the emperor. It was a period for advances in cultural and scientific achievements and a time to create a unified Chinese identity. Over the Silk Road trade route, Buddhism, the most important religion from outside China, came to the country from India around A.D. 65. Buddhism brought new ideas to China, including the concepts of *nirvana* (heavenly bliss) and reincarnation. By A.D. 700, Buddhism, Taoism, and Confucianism all coexisted in China.

The Han period saw great territorial expansion. The empire reached to the present-day Xinjiang Autonomous Region in the far west, Korea in the east, and Vietnam in the south. For the first time, the Chinese empire bore some spatial relation to its modern-day state and territorial limits. The population grew to about 60 million.

The river basins of central and eastern China, with their large tracts of arable land, have always been the economic base for the Chinese state. This area sustained a large farming population. The north and west borderlands, however, were controlled only with great difficulty. Even today, the Tibetans and the Uighur Muslims continually contest Chinese rule in Tibet and the Xinjiang Autonomous Region, respectively.

Fifteen emperors ruled during the Han period. As in earlier imperial dynasties, change came through uprisings and revolts. After the end of the Han period, a number of kingdoms and dynasties arose, held and fought for power, and collapsed. This period of disunity lasted for nearly 400 years from A.D. 220 to 589.

SUI DYNASTY

The Sui Dynasty (A.D. 590–618) attempted to consolidate China and rebuild parts of the Great Wall. The Sui emperor also simplified and strengthened the bureaucracy, adopted a new legal code, and created a palace city near Xian. The dynasty's greatest construction feat was the completion of the Grand Canal. This was an important south-north link, as it connected to several major waterways from Hangzhou north to Beijing.

TANG DYNASTY

The seventh century marked the start of the medieval period in Chinese history. Chinese culture reached a refined and cosmopolitan level—literature, art, music, and agriculture flourished. Under the Tang Dynasty (618–907), China expanded. The Turkish empires were defeated, and the Tibetans became reliable allies. Mercantile cities, such as Guangzhou in the Pearl River delta near Hong Kong, were influenced by Islam. During the Tang period, the Uighurs, a Turkic-speaking people, created their own empire in central Asia, northern Xinjiang, and parts of Mongolia. They decided to ally with the Tang government rather than confront it.

The Tang dynasty witnessed the only woman in Chinese history to become a reigning empress. Empress Wu was a dominant power for 20 years (A.D. 684–704). She was a great supporter of Buddhism and commissioned the famous Longmen Buddhist cliff carvings outside Luoyang, 185 miles (300 km) east of the ancient capital of Xian. The 2,000 caves are shallow openings in the limestone cliffs where 100,000 Buddhist statues were carved, including a Buddha that is 56 feet (17 m) high.

SONG DYNASTY

Finally, in A.D. 960, the Northern and Southern Song dynasties emerged for a 300-year period. The northern part of the country was well connected to the Grand Canal so that it could bring in grain from the south. The country became economically advanced, and industry and technology blossomed. Overseas commerce added greatly to the government's revenues. Gunpowder, the magnetic compass, fine porcelain,

and movable type printing were invented and used. Preoc-
cupation with the arts and science probably caused a military
decline, which eventually made the country vulnerable to the
thirteenth-century Mongol invasion.

MONGOL (YUAN) DYNASTY

The period from 1279 to 1368 saw significant parts of China
fall under foreign domination. The Mongols from the north
breached the Great Wall and began their conquest in the
thirteenth century. By 1279, the Mongol (Yuan) Dynasty had
begun its reign.

The rule of the famous Kublai Khan (1215–1294) set the
tone for this dynasty. Beijing was selected as the capital, and
influence spread to Korea and as far west as Tibet and Burma.
Between 1271 and 1292, the explorer Marco Polo made his
journeys to China. For 17 years, he resided in Beijing, opening
the way to foreign influence.

MING DYNASTY

From 1356 to 1382, Mongol rule weakened, and the Ming
Dynasty was founded in 1368. It lasted almost 300 years. The
early Ming emperors were forward-looking and worked hard to
rule and hold their power. They rebuilt the Great Wall, rerouted
the Grand Canal to end near Beijing, and built a new southern
capital at Nanjing. Early on, they established a powerful navy
and sent out maritime expeditions of diplomacy and exploration. From 1405 to 1433, Chinese explorers went to the South
China Sea, to Ceylon (now Sri Lanka) and India, to the Persian
Gulf and to coastal East Africa, including Kenya and the offshore island of Zanzibar. Research suggests that China's most
famous navigator, Admiral Zheng He (1371–1435), possibly
completed the first circumnavigation of the world, beating
Portuguese explorer Ferdinand Magellan by a century. Zheng,
a Muslim eunuch, commanded a fleet of 300 ships and some
30,000 sailors.

Included in the fleet were enormous "treasure ships." These were 400 feet (122 m) long and 160 feet (49 m) wide, with 9 masts, 12 sails, and numerous decks. The world had never seen an armada like the Ming ships. One of these great ships was nearly twice as long as the combined length of the three ships that Columbus sailed across the Atlantic Ocean in 1492.

The Chinese expeditions, however, were cut short in 1433. After a change in government, the new bureaucracy considered them a waste of money and resources. The Ming Dynasty withdrew from sea voyages and even banned coastal shipping for more than 150 years. Had they decided to continue to explore by sea, they had such strong potential for foreign colonization that the map of the world might have changed before Columbus had even been born.

Instead, more foreigners began to come to China. In 1514, Portuguese vessels sailed to the Pearl River delta, and in 1557, the Macau enclave was formed. This colonial outpost remained under Portuguese control for more than 450 years, until the Chinese assumed sovereignty over the territory in December 1999. The Ming Dynasty also saw a wave of Christian missionaries, as the Jesuits came to China between 1582 and 1610.

MANCHU (QING) DYNASTY

After the 300-year Ming rule, the Manchus from Manchuria gradually conquered China and established the Qing Dynasty (1644–1911). The Qing was the last of the dynasties, bringing China into the twentieth century. The Manchus added Inner and Outer Mongolia, Tibet, Turkestan, and Taiwan to the empire's territories. During the latter part of Manchu rule, the British East India Company expanded. In 1793, Great Britain tried to establish trade relations with China, but the Chinese emperor, Chien Lung, saw no benefit in trade with England. After that refusal, a secret market was established in China for western goods, especially the drug opium. This led to the Opium War (1839–1842), which brought China into conflict with British troops. China wanted its own control over trade with the West. The 1842 Treaty of Nanking was signed after China's defeat. China paid a heavy price for losing this war. Several treaty ports were forced to open to British residents, and China subsequently lost Hong Kong to Great Britain.

Anti-Manchu forces protesting economic hardships caused the Taiping Rebellion of 1850–1864. Government troops, along with paid foreign troops, defeated the rebels. Twenty million Chinese died between 1850 and 1870 in prolonged fighting and economic disorder.

The mother of Emperor Tsai Chun, known unofficially as Empress Dowager Cixi, held the real power and ruled from behind the scenes from 1861 to 1908. The Qing Dynasty declined quickly. Under pressure from European powers and a newly risen Japan, the Chinese Empire was shrinking fast. Chinese dependencies such as Vietnam (Annan) and Burma were lost, as was Chinese territory in eastern Siberia, parts of Manchuria, and the island of Taiwan. The principal beneficiaries were France, Great Britain, Russia, and Japan.

In the 1890s, China was in chaos. Foreign powers competed with one another to gain concessions from China. Economic hardship led the common people to protest in uprisings. The most serious was the anti-foreign Boxer Uprising of 1900, which led to a disastrous war and the occupation of the Chinese capital of Peking by the joint military forces of eight foreign nations. Peace was restored only after China signed a humiliating treaty. The Qing Dynasty lingered on for another decade until a revolution led by Dr. Sun Yat-sen toppled it in 1912.

THE REPUBLIC

A Chinese republic was founded in 1912, but the process of decline and political disintegration of the Qing Dynasty continued. Mongolia and Tibet declared their independence from China. The rest of the country was soon plunged into incessant civil wars fought among military strongmen. The next 16 years, from 1912 to 1928, are known as "the warlord period" in Chinese history. Regional warlords often ignored the central government, as foreign powers took even greater control away from China. Another wave of revolution swept the country, led by the Nationalist Party founded by Sun Yat-sen in temporary alliance with the Chinese Communist Party. In 1928, the Nationalists defeated the warlords and set up a new central government under Chiang Kai-shek, the successor to Sun. This Nationalist government, with its capital at Nanking, ruled China until 1949, interrupted by a bitter war against Japanese invasions that lasted from 1937 to 1945.

COMMUNIST MAO ERA

The long war against Japan sapped the energy and exhausted the resources of the Nationalist government. On the other hand, the Communist Party, now under the leadership of Mao Zedong, expanded rapidly during the war years because of its ability to win the support of the millions of people living in wretched conditions. Mao appealed mostly to Chinese peasants with the simple slogan, "Land to the tiller." After the Japanese surrender in 1945, the Communists challenged the Nationalist government and gained control of mainland China in 1949. The defeated Nationalists were forced to flee to the island of Taiwan, which had only recently been freed from 50 years of Japanese colonial rule.

The new Communist regime called itself the People's Republic of China and made Beijing (Peking) its capital. As chairman of the party, Mao Zedong became the absolute ruler of China for nearly 30 years. During the first eight years, 1949 to 1957, the People's Republic of China made an alliance with the Soviet Union, intervened in support of North Korea in the Korean War, and consolidated its control over the entire Chinese mainland, including the frontier regions of Inner Mongolia, Xinjiang, and Tibet. It restored peace in the country,

Mao Zedong, the leader of the Communist revolution in China, overthrew the Nationalist government after World War II and renamed the country the People's Republic of China. Mao implemented reforms and policies that led to major changes but also widespread famine, cultural and social upheaval, and general chaos throughout China.

pursued policies of economic rehabilitation and development, and carried out the first stage of its "socialist revolution" by eliminating rural landlords and urban capitalists.

Relative success in domestic and foreign policies led Mao and his supporters in the party to pursue a more radical approach over the next 20 years to revolutionize China's economic and social structure. Campaigns to launch the so-called Great Leap Forward in economic production and to set up People's Communes to incorporate all the rural peasant population resulted in great disasters. Human policy errors, combined with unfavorable natural conditions in 1959 and 1960, caused widespread famine. An estimated 20 million to 30 million people died during this time. The government parted ways from its Communist ally, the Soviet Union, in the 1950s and began to challenge both the United States and the Soviet Union for leadership in the world, particularly among underdeveloped countries. Chinese-Soviet relations reached a breaking point in 1969 when the two Communist giants fought a series of border clashes.

In 1966, Mao and his followers launched the Cultural Revolution with the avowed goal of establishing ideological purity for the Chinese people. An intense power struggle marked this period as Mao sought to purge his political rivals, real or imagined. Millions of people came under political persecution, and industrial and agricultural production suffered major decline. The "10 disastrous years" of the Cultural Revolution ended only with Mao's death and the purge of the radicals in late 1976. Even before the Cultural Revolution came to an end, however, China made a major shift in foreign policy. It allowed President Richard Nixon of the United States to visit China in February 1972 and paved the way for the two countries to have normal diplomatic relations. China also began diplomatic relations with other Western powers and gained admission to the United Nations General Assembly, replacing Taiwan as a permanent member of the Security Council in 1971.

POST-MAO PERIOD

A new leadership emerged in China after 1976 with the rise of the pragmatic Deng Xiaoping. While the Communist Party maintained its monopoly on political power, Deng's economic policy marked a sharp departure from Mao. He promoted reform in various sectors of the economy, promoted growth in foreign trade, and opened China for foreign investment. The success of the reform led to rapid economic growth in the 1980s and 1990s. China began to emerge as an economic powerhouse.

Such drastic change in the economy inevitably affected China's social and political structure. Rising discontent with official corruption and inflation, coupled with the growing demand for democracy, brought about massive student demonstrations at Tiananmen Square in Beijing during the spring and summer of 1989. The government treated this as a form of social protest and called out the military to suppress the demonstrators by force. The clash resulted in the deaths of hundreds of student demonstrators. Such disregard for human rights was widely condemned, and the international community ostracized China. However, China's leaders made no change to the policy of economic reform and the opening to the outside world. Gradually, the nation's economic strength won back the favor of foreign countries.

Through the end of the twentieth century and the start of the twenty-first, China has pursued a good-neighbor foreign policy. The fall of the Soviet Union in 1991 made it easier for China to restore cordial relations with Russia and other new states in central Asia. Hong Kong and Macau were returned to Chinese sovereignty. An unresolved problem is the continued existence of independent Taiwan, which is still outside of China's jurisdiction. Despite growing ties in trade, investment, and cultural exchange between the two sides, the issue of Taiwan continues to be a tension point of potentially major magnitude.

In recognition of China's new status in the world, Beijing won the right to host the 2008 Summer Olympics. More than 11,000 athletes from 204 nations and territories competed in the Games. China won the most gold medals (51) and was second only to the United States in terms of overall medals. For the Chinese, the broad success of the Games provided evidence that China had finally overcome the "national humiliation" caused by Western interference in its affairs since the early nineteenth century.

The World Trade Organization finally extended China full membership in 2001. Becoming a member of the WTO ensured that China's fast-growing economy would have equal status with the economies of other world powers. China is working to create a capitalist, market-oriented economy within a Communist framework of government. The imperial dynasties, which lasted thousands of years, have disappeared to give China a new orientation for the twenty-first century. Such a change would hardly have been contemplated just 50 years ago.

4

People and Culture

W ith more than 1.3 billion people, China contains more than one-fifth of the world's population. There are nearly five times as many people in the country as in the United States. And the number of people is expected to climb to 1.437 billion people by 2050. China's population is both a resource and a continuing problem and concern.

POPULATION

Two significant population trends are likely to occur in China. The first trend is the aging of the population. By 2025, more than 300 million people will be over age 60. It is projected that this age group will make up some 20 percent of the population. The second trend involves the urban population, which has already grown from 20 percent in 1950 to slightly more than 45 percent in 2008. It is expected to account for 55 percent of the population by 2025 or before. Thus, urban areas will continue to grow and become increasingly overcrowded. The southern province of Guangdong, the eastern provinces of Henan and Shandong, and the central province of Sichuan are the most populated ones in the country. The first three have more than 93 million people and Sichuan has more than 82 million. Chongqing in Sichuan is one of the four directly-administered municipalities in China and is administratively the largest city in the world, with more than 30 million people in its municipal region. (The boundaries of the Chongqing municipality extend farther into rural areas than for most cities; the population of the urban area of Chongqing is 6 million.) China has 10 cities with populations of 4 million or more. By 2025, the country's urban population could reach 800 million.

Coupled with the rise in urbanization is the continuing movement of large numbers of rural people to the cities. These migrants have formed the bulk of the labor force central to urban construction and factory expansion during the past decade. Even with the economic dislocation of 2008–2009, China plans to expand some 600 towns into cities by 2011. The social and municipal cost of this population shift is a major concern to Chinese urban planners.

China's population density is 358 people per square mile (138 per sq km), but this figure needs regional interpretation. Each of the 11 coastal provinces, from Guangxi in the south to Liaoning in the north, has an average population density of 992 people per square mile (383 per sq km). For nine centrally located provinces, from Hunan in the south to Heilongjiang, including Inner Mongolia, in the north, the average drops to a third of that. Each of the remaining nine western region provinces has only 140 people per square mile (55 per sq km). The United States has approximately 75 people per square mile (29 per sq km). Chinese cities average about 26,000 people per square mile (10,000 per sq km).

In 2007, China created 12 million new jobs—more than the population of Greece—shaving urban unemployment to 4 percent, but pressures remain as 10 million more people enter the workforce in the world's most populous nation annually. Above, people gather to inquire about jobs at an employment fair in Hefei in eastern China.

The distribution of China's population is highly uneven and generally reflects the country's climatic patterns—especially the availability of water. Ninety-five percent of China's population resides in China Proper, the humid eastern region. This part of the country has 43 percent of China's land area and most of the prime agricultural land. A closer look reveals that 80 percent of China's population lives in the four major river basins: the Northeast Plain, or the Liao-Songhua River Basin; the lower Huang He (Yellow River) Basin, or North China Plain; the upper and lower basins of the Chang Jiang (Yangtze River); and the Xi (West) and Pearl River basin of south China. Essentially, population densities are high along the coast, remain high along major river valleys westward, and gradually decrease farther inland. One exception is the inland Sichuan Basin of the Chang Jiang. Estimated population density for the basin is 1,295 people per square mile (500 per sq km). In the far west, such as on the Tibetan Plateau, there are fewer than 26 people per square mile (10 per sq km), and there are broad regions with only an average of 2 people per square mile (less than 1 per sq km).

Though the Chinese population has grown steadily over the centuries, it increased dramatically during the first two decades of Communist rule. During the years of Mao's rule, the population increased because birth control was thought to be anti-Communist and because Marxist philosophy encouraged more workers for the production of more economic goods. After Mao's death in 1976, family-planning programs became strict, with the government promoting a rigid, one-child-per-family rule. Because of the one-child policy, China's projected growth rate for 2001–2050 is only 8 percent, compared with an estimated 58 percent in India, which has no family-planning policy. The Chinese government introduced a complex system of economic rewards to help achieve this one-child family. These incentives included better living conditions, extra grain rations, and improved education and employment opportunities for the single child. Parents with two or more children faced fines and abortion threats, and consequently, they would sometimes abandon a girl child, who was less desirable in Chinese society.

Traditionally, Asian societies, including the Chinese, favor male children. This sentiment is more often the case in rural areas, where males are seen as more productive in agricultural work. The gender ratio varies, depending on region, from 105 to more than 125 boys for every 100 girls born. The world average is 105 boys to 100 girls. Obviously, a one-child society and a growing elderly population will mean a greater responsibility for both the government and the single child. In 2007, there were more than 140 million Chinese over the age of 60. Historically this senior population would have been cared for in extended families. But the single-child policy of the last 30 years has profoundly changed Chinese demographic patterns. It has thrown new responsibilities on urban governments to care for the elderly who have no children to live with.

In China, 19 percent of the population is younger than 15, compared with the world figure of 30 percent. This means that there are 250 million Chinese youth who need education and have hopes for jobs and careers in their future. The literacy rate for youth in China is 99 percent, and this further increases their level of ambition and desire for opportunities. To give some sense of the scale of change in Communist China, the average life expectancy in 1950 was 41. In 2009 it was 71.6 for men and 75.5 for women.

LANGUAGE

The language of China is the most widely spoken native tongue on Earth. Although spoken dialects are different, the language shares the same writing system, with the exception of the scripts used by notable ethnic minorities, such as the Uighurs, Kazaks, Tibetans, and Mongols. In the late 1950s, the government tried to simplify the language. It adopted the so-called pinyin system of standard Chinese. It is based on the pronunciation of the Chinese characters in northern Mandarin and the Chinese spoken in the Beijing region.

Mandarin is the language used in government, schools, radio, television, and movies. It has become the language most frequently spoken in large urban centers.

Other major dialects are Cantonese (or Yue), spoken in southern China and Hong Kong; Wu, spoken in Shanghai and the nearby provinces of eastern China; and Min, spoken in southeast China. The Cantonese dialect is quite widespread and is generally favored in Chinese communities overseas, including parts of Southeast Asia and the West.

The great majority of Chinese traveled little in the past, even within their own provinces. This lack of contact between the regions has allowed language diversity to develop. Thus, a wide variation of dialects exists even within provinces.

ETHNIC PICTURE

China views itself as a thoroughly unified country. In large part, this is because the Han people, who account for approximately 92 percent of the population, consider themselves to be the original Chinese people. They trace their lineage as far back as the Han Dynasty of 206 B.C. The Han live mainly in central and eastern China. They are also widely scattered in north-central China and across the Tibetan Plateau. The Han account for more than 90 percent of the population in 19 of the 22 provinces.

A total of some 90 million people belong to 55 minority ethnic groups. Fifteen of these minorities comprise 90 percent of the ethnic minority population. The government has given some minorities special administrative status. These minorities are officially recognized, and their language and customs are somewhat encouraged. At the highest political level of recognition, the government has established autonomous regions. These autonomous regions occupy the border areas of the country and are strategically located. There are five autonomous regions, and each has a dominant minority.

In the far west, the Tibetans in Xizang and the Uighurs (the country's third-largest minority) in Xinjiang comprise two of the autonomous regions. In the north, the Mongols in Inner Mongolia and the Hui (the country's second-largest minority) in Ningxia comprise two other autonomous regions. China's largest ethnic minority, the Zhuang in Guangxi, in the southwest, occupies the fifth autonomous region.

It should be noted that three of the five autonomous regions are in large, sparsely populated areas. These are China's frontier border regions and act as buffer zones. Tibet is a buffer with Burma (Myanmar), India, Bhutan, and Nepal. Xinjiang is a buffer with Pakistan, Afghanistan, Tajikistan, Kyrgyzstan, Kazakhstan, and for 25 miles (40 km) with Russia in the extreme northwest. Inner Mongolia is a buffer with Mongolia and Russia's Far East.

The autonomous regions guarantee political equality for minority groups. Yet in some cases, Chinese rule has been fiercely contested. Two noted examples of such conflicts involve followers of the Dalai Lama in Tibet and the millions of Uighur Muslims in Xinjiang. At times, Uighur nationalists have detonated bombs in Beijing and in the provincial capital, Urumqi. In March 2008, riots broke out in Lhasa, the capital of Tibet, as Tibetans attacked Han Chinese living and working in the city. The riot, which resulted in 19 deaths, led to a government crackdown in the autonomous region. In Urumqi, ethnic clashes broke out in July 2009 between the Uighurs and the Han Chinese, killing almost 200 people.

The Chinese government has pressed the minority people to learn Mandarin Chinese if they want advancement and employment outside their villages. Still, many minority groups prefer to maintain their distinct cultures, languages, and religions. This continually poses problems for the central government.

RELIGION

Religious beliefs have profoundly influenced Chinese society from the earliest times. Confucianism, Taoism, and the assimilation of Buddhism from India helped to create the rich and unique system of thought that has structured Chinese society for more than 2,000 years. The western religions of Islam and Christianity have made inroads over the last 1,300 years.

Chinese religion has tended to be centered on the family and the local community. Taoism, founded in the sixth century B.C., promotes oneness and harmony with nature as a way of life. It can involve meditation, philosophical debate, and magic. Taoists deeply influenced Chinese arts, particularly painting and poetry.

One of the major ethnic minority groups in China, the Uighur Muslims, struggles with the authority of the Chinese government. Many believe the Communist government suppresses Uighur language, culture, and religion, and several Uighur political groups have demanded independence to create their own nation. Above, Uighur craftsmen sharpen knives in Xinjiang Province.

Related to Taoist ideas is the concept of *yin* and *yang*, the two opposing forces believed to be present in all of nature. This is the idea of dark and light, or winter and summer.

Confucianism, more a philosophy than a religion, was also founded in the sixth century B.C. It is more involved with government workings and interpersonal relationships. One of its aims was to promote an ethical society, placing emphasis on the dignity of the human being.

Buddhism, a foreign religion from India, stresses the idea of becoming an enlightened being, or bodhisattva, by breaking the cycle of desire, suffering, and rebirth. Buddhist ideas have had a strong influence on Chinese culture, including art, architecture, poetry, and fiction. Followers of Buddhism in China have faced hardships. During the 1950s and the Cultural Revolution period of 1966–1976, thousands of Buddhist monasteries were closed. In Tibet alone, 6,000 monasteries were shut down or destroyed, and only 25 remained after the destructive decade of the Cultural Revolution.

The early Communist period was a time of anti-religious policies, and damage was inflicted on temples, monasteries, churches, mosques, and other religious buildings. In effect, religion was forced underground. The Communist leader Mao Zedong was elevated to a godlike status. His portrait and statues are still found in public and private places. For example, his painted portrait, prominently displayed at the entrance to the Forbidden City in Beijing, overlooks Tiananmen Square. His face is also pictured on the 100-yuan bill. Mao's influence was especially promoted during the Cultural Revolution. During this time, all books were devoted to Mao's thoughts and sayings. Among them was the Little Red Book, *Quotations from Chairman Mao.* Recently, religious beliefs have begun to be practiced more openly, yet the government still monitors such activities closely.

ART AND POPULAR CULTURE

Chinese culture has a rich artistic and intellectual heritage. A great array of historians, writers, poets, artists, and musicians made great contributions to the culture over the centuries. Such developments as calligraphy (which means "beautiful writing"), painting, the care of gardens with miniature trees (bonsai), and the keeping of ornamental fish and birds add to the richness of the culture. Elderly men still gather in local parks to enjoy their caged birds and socialize.

Chinese culture is perhaps best shown in the tremendous variety of ideas and inventions that first appeared in China, which include the seismograph, the magnetic compass, silk, gunpowder, paper, fireworks, porcelain, the suspension bridge, the horse collar, and the crank handle. Many of these inventions did not appear in the West for centuries after they appeared in China. For example, the wheelbarrow took 9 to 10 centuries after being developed in China to reach the West; canal lock gates, 7 to 17 centuries; gunpowder, 5 to 6 centuries; and paper, 10 centuries. The Silk Road helped disperse these Chinese inventions to the West.

Also from China came important medical discoveries, such as blood circulation, the thyroid hormone, smallpox immunology, acupuncture treatment, and deficiency diseases. The Chinese, as well, have always excelled at mathematics, and many of their discoveries are well known in the Western world.

As Chinese society becomes more urban, traditional culture gives way to big-city life. Exposure to foreign influence—fast-food outlets like McDonald's and Kentucky Fried Chicken, drinks like Pepsi and Coca-Cola, and Western music, fashions, and electronic gadgets—make for a changing culture. China had some 700 million cell phones and 300 million Internet users by the end of 2008. Not all people favor these trends.

Family is still of major importance in Chinese culture. Most children live in a close, loving family structure. Generally, Asian societies treat a young person up to about age eight as a "Golden Child," who can do almost no wrong. Chinese society is also concerned about preserving hierarchy. Status in the family hierarchy is always foremost. The Chinese extended family encourages elderly parents to assist and influence family life. The effects of any disgrace touch even the extended family. The concept of honor, or "saving face," is important. As a result, disagreements are best settled in private.

LITERATURE

Some Western writers suggest that certain difficulties hinder the enjoyment of Chinese literature and poetry. The Chinese language itself and its translation into other languages are obvious barriers. One needs a vocabulary of more than 5,000

Chinese characters and an intimate understanding of Chinese history and literature to appreciate the subtle nuances of what is written, particularly in Chinese classical poetry.

Traditional Chinese literature is closely linked with Confucius. The recorded words of Confucius and his disciples, known as the Confucian Classics, were considered a beneficial influence on society and the state. The Classics became the basis of education in traditional China. To gain entrance to the Chinese governmental bureaucracy—a keenly sought-after lifetime position—one had to master the Classics.

A second category of traditional literature includes historical writings. Few other nations are as aware of their history as China. The first general comprehensive history was compiled around 100 B.C. It contained political, social, economic, cultural, and physical geographic records from antiquity to the Han Dynasty. Later, historians focused on a particular dynastic period rather than general history. In total, 24 "official histories" were compiled by the end of the eighteenth century, unquestionably the most voluminous historical records of any country.

The third category is made up of philosophical works. Philosophers and intellectuals of various schools of thought wrote these from ancient times to the early modern period.

The final category includes literary works. Among these is a variety of collected works of poems, essays, literary treatises, and personal letters. Poetry, because of its creativity in expressing deep feelings, has always been an appreciated and honored form of literature in China.

There is also a specialized geographic literature. *Fangzhi*, or gazetteers, were documents that date back to the Han Dynasty (circa 200 B.C.). They were local geographies of places ranging in size from villages to larger administrative districts. The Fangzhi dealt with the founding of a city, economic activities, political boundaries, customs, and local gentry. They often had maps as well. These works have been treasures for people researching the origins and development of specific places in China and the networks of Chinese historical geography.

In traditional China, success depended on an educated person's mastery of these literary works. The Chinese civil service was based on a series of examinations that tested a candidate's knowledge of literature and ability in literary composition.

Later literary developments included drama, opera, and fiction. At first, these works were not considered respectable because the narrative and dialogue used everyday vocabulary, not the literary style needed to achieve social status. Eventually, such works became an accepted form of literature.

SOCIETY AND HEALTH

Health and food are important cultural concerns for the Chinese. Cities have Western medical facilities as well as traditional Chinese medical clinics. The traditional approach is a holistic one, which takes into account the entire body rather than a single complaint. Many herbal remedies are used to treat a wide variety of ailments. One widely practiced traditional technique is acupuncture. Needles are inserted at specific points on the body, each of which is thought to be linked through circulation to a particular organ.

Many Chinese maintain their health by the practice of *tai ji*, also known as *tai chi*. These exercises are practiced throughout China in public places in the early morning hours. They are generally engaged in by the elderly, who hope to maintain flexibility through slow graceful movements in a ballet-like dance.

One health issue facing China and other Asian societies arises from tobacco smoking. Since the 1980s, the amount of farmland used to grow tobacco in China has tripled. The country imports and exports tobacco on a large scale. Estimates are that one in every three cigarettes smoked in the world today is smoked in China. By 2050, it is thought that smoking will kill more than 8,000 people each day in the country, most of them

A popular exercise among middle-aged and elderly people in China, tai chi consists of a series of fluid postures and movements that help reduce stress and increase muscle, flexibility, and energy.

men. It is said that the biggest cigarette company in the world is the Chinese government. Tobacco contributes up to 10 percent of total government revenues. The government is beginning to pay attention to the harmful effects of tobacco and may take action to improve the situation.

The Chinese have a great love of food. China is home to one of the world's great cuisines, featuring many regional cooking styles. The four major regional styles are northern (Beijing), southern (Cantonese), coastal (Shanghai), and inland (Sichuan). Vegetarian food is popular, with rice an ever-present staple. Rice and wheat flour are served in various forms—grain, noodles, or dumpling wrappers. Meats include pork, beef, fish, and fowl. Other foods on display at restaurants include live snakes and seafood. Custom says that it is best to eat meat immediately after it is killed and cooked. In the past, lack of refrigeration led to this practice. Chinese youth today are more often opting for a Western-style diet, and over the years, they have dramatically increased their consumption of meat, as well as their body weight.

Research suggests that tea originated in China, or was introduced to China from Southeast Asia, some 2,000 years ago. Over the centuries, tea became an integral part of the culture, and teahouses grew in large numbers. Tea brewing and drinking has become a ceremony in itself. The teacup in China is seen everywhere, like the coffee mug in North America. Many tea varieties reflect regional variations and preferences. In 2006, China produced more than one million tons of tea, making it the world's leading producer.

Beer is also a popular drink in China, rivaling tea as a preferred beverage. During the nineteenth century, Germans established the first brewery in coastal Qingdao, in Shandong Province. The Tsingtao (Qingdao) label is the most popular. However, every province in China produces its own brand of beer. In some areas, beer is cheaper than bottled water.

Chinese culture has endured for many centuries. It is rich, complex, unique, innovative, and enduring. Many Western observers have only a superficial knowledge and understanding of this culture, which will likely continue to flourish and deepen its historical roots, even in light of the strong influences of the Western world.

5

Government and Politics

China has been a cultural unit for several thousand years. The exact limits of the Chinese Empire, however, have varied over the centuries. Control of the territory has sometimes been strong and widespread, but it has also been weak and fragmented at other times.

TRADITIONAL GOVERNMENT

The organization of broad areas of China into a political state dates from at least 1500 B.C. By then, Chinese society had developed a unique writing system. This early historical state was centered east of present-day Xian on the fertile soils of the middle Huang He Valley.

China was first unified as a nation-state under the rule of the first Qin emperor in 221 B.C. Since that time, China has generally had a strong, unified state headed by a single, powerful ruler. The Chinese divide their history based on the reigns of the various emperors of the ruling dynasties. If rulers were just, fair, and effective, they received widespread support. Improper or ineffective rule or corruption, as shown by poor harvests or losses in battles or because of natural disasters, led the rulers to lose this support. A new dynasty would then emerge.

Each dynasty functioned as a state and could extract substantial revenues and labor from large populations. The bureaucratic system worked remarkably well and functioned without much major change for 2,000 years from its founding in the third century B.C. to its fall in 1911. The key thread was the idea of a unified state with a strong central government led by a single ruler exercising direct control over local governments and neighboring lesser states. Deviations from a central imperial form of government were only evident in some five of the 20 centuries of China's political history. The persistence of the Chinese Empire, however chaotic and fractured at times, is the most impressive feat of the Chinese political tradition.

Social order was maintained from the imperial throne down through bureaucratic officials, the scholar-gentry, to the commoners, who included peasant-farmers, artisan-craftsmen, and merchants. There was a careful division of labor and a balance of power and authority for all sectors. All social classes were tied together by the ideas of Confucianism, which stressed harmony in human relations beginning with the family and radiating outward to expanding worlds of responsibility, resulting in social cohesion and order. From the Han Dynasty (206 B.C.–A.D. 220) onward, Confucianism was institutionalized as an ideological foundation of government and prevailed in principle for 2,000 years. This was the beginning of the Chinese bureaucratic tradition. Educated people studied for imperial examinations, and if they passed, they were granted government posts. Examinations stressed knowledge of the Confucian Classics, so certain specific rituals governed the

Surrounded by imperial gardens on three sides, the south side of the Forbidden City in Beijing features Tiananmen Gate *(above)*, the entrance to the imperial city, and Tiananmen Square. Frequently used for public celebrations, Tiananmen Square has also been the location of some of China's most controversial events.

bureaucracy through the centuries. Examinations, which were open to anyone, were seen as the best way to move up in society. They were based on knowledge, ability, and a belief in traditional bureaucratic structure.

Great attention was given to ritual and ceremony in conducting state business. These imperial institutions were designed to reflect a sense of awesome power and unapproachable remoteness from the people. The heavily guarded Forbidden City, or Imperial City in Beijing, allowed the emperor to conduct daily affairs away from the prying eyes of common people. The Forbidden City itself symbolized the emperor's unique position at the center of the universe. This palatial complex (said to have 5,000 rooms) is considered the incarnation of the celestial palace on Earth.

All imperial processions were conducted with an air of sacred splendor and dignified isolation. Traditional values and ritual symbolism followed from dynasty to dynasty. This is why stability re-emerged after prolonged periods of chaos, conflict, and division.

The Ming emperors, 1368–1644, employed more than 70,000 eunuchs in their bureaucracy. Eunuchs were castrated male attendants whose official job was to supervise daily business in the palace, including the oversight of the women of the court. Eunuchs were used in Chinese courts for more than 2,000 years, but they reached the zenith of their power during the Ming Dynasty, serving as important links between the inner imperial world and the outer bureaucratic world. By the 1590s, they played a central role in the political life of China, collecting revenues in the provinces, using military guards to terrorize wealthy families, controlling food supplies, and even writing historical works.

Money was an important part of dynastic rule. It was needed to maintain an extensive bureaucracy and to keep a well-trained army that would defend and oversee a large empire. Taxation of the people was necessary. To lessen tax demands on citizens, it was important to produce an agricultural surplus above the subsistence level. Dynasties often failed because of waste, extravagance, and heavy taxes. The power of an emperor could decline if provincial bureaucrats gained local support and functioned independently. Any economic improvement, such as the Grand Canal of the seventh century or an upswing in rice production, was important in raising tax money to feed the military's armies.

All dynasties had to maintain effective communication and transportation between the central government and the frontiers. Foot runners, horses, and boats were all part of a government courier system. Effective government rule required an efficient transportation system, including canals, bridges, and roads.

Maximum territorial control was first established under the Tang Dynasty, A.D. 618–907. It was impossible, however, to control such a vast territory for long. Extension of territory always meant that loyal government officials and soldiers had to be present in the outer regions to oversee and secure government business. In times of peace, soldiers doubled as farmers. The soldier-farmer was key to keeping territory under control and united. The idea was to have self-sufficient garrisons, even in semiarid regions. Military settlements were walled for protection.

The physical character of China's boundaries allowed any given dynasty to maintain strong rule, assuming there was domestic tranquility. The eastern seaboard, the rain forests of the southeast, and the western and southern mountain ranges were formidable barriers for any outside penetration of the territory. The only foreign intrusions came from the north and northwest, where open country allowed troops to move more easily. Historically, nomadic tribes, such as the Huns, Turks, Mongols, and Manchus, all invaded China from that region.

The rise of independent regional military power was always a concern for a dynasty. Army personnel would be moved from one location to another to prevent generals from cultivating local power and support, which might allow political fragmentation. At times, this constant change made the troops less effective and the dynasty more vulnerable to a new political regime or outside influences.

The Ming (1368–1644) and Qing (1644–1911) dynasties each showed great political skill in maintaining imperial unity for more than two centuries. Part of this success was achieved because of firearms. By rebuilding the Great Wall with fixed cannons, the Ming emperors also resisted invasions from the north for more than a century and a half. The Grand Canal was used effectively to move military supplies, as well as surplus grains, with wheat to the south and rice to the north. Thus, the Ming dynasty had a proven and effectively deployed army. The succeeding Qing Dynasty simply allowed the army to continue as before. This helped in the annexation of parts of Outer China and vast areas in the northwest.

Two thousand years of dynastic rule has strongly influenced more recent governments in China. The present Communist form of government is in many ways similar to dynastic rule: There is one strong leader, a bureaucracy, and a large, well-trained army. Communism has been in place for only 60 years, and it is already undergoing major modifications and transitions, particularly since Deng Xiaoping initiated sweeping economic reforms in the late 1970s.

CONTEMPORARY GOVERNMENT

Today, the government of China is under the control of a single party, the Chinese Communist Party (CCP). A few other so-called democratic parties are allowed to exist, but they are largely deprived of political power. The Communist Party, with a membership of more than 73 million in 2007, is spread across 3.3 million local branches. It is the world's largest political organization and dominates the political, economic, and social life of the nation. Those who lead the party formulate policies for the entire country. The party's role is not confined only to politics and ideology, but it also extends to all aspects of life, including industry, commerce, agriculture, education, social organization, and the military. The party controls all major appointments, and most leading officials are party members. A unit of the party oversees every major branch of the Chinese government.

China's Communist Party is highly centralized. In theory, local party members elect representatives to form county party committees. Members of the county committees elect representatives to the provincial party committees. In turn, members of the provincial committees elect representatives to attend the National Party Congress, which meets once every five years. A Central Committee consists of up to 200 members and is elected by the Congress. It is responsible for policy-making and the approval of major personnel appointments. Because the Central Committee meets only a few times a year, it elects a Political Bureau (Politburo) of two dozen members to take charge of important party affairs. The Politburo, and particularly its seven-member standing committee, contains the most powerful leaders of China. All members of the Politburo and most in the Central Committee serve concurrently in the top positions of the government. For instance, Hu Jintao holds the country's top three political positions: general secretary of the Communist Party, president of People's Republic of China, and chair of the Central Military Commission. The general secretary of the party is also chair at meetings of the Politburo and the Central Committee.

The Chinese government is a pyramid bureaucratic organization parallel to the party structure. The president heads the central government, located in the capital of Beijing. The executive branch of the government is the State Council, which is led by the premier and several vice premiers. The State Council consists of more than 30 ministries and commissions. It is similar in size to the cabinet of a country like the United States, Russia, or India. A court system headed by the Supreme Court forms the judicial branch. The National People's Congress, with thousands of members chosen by electoral districts throughout the country and nationwide professional associations, meets once a year at the capital. In theory, it has the power to approve major legislation and personnel appointments made by the State Council.

Ever since Mao Zedong's rise to power in 1949, the Chinese Communist Party has controlled the Chinese government. After a period of reforms in the 1970s, China has experienced an enormous amount of economic growth. President Hu Jintao (*above*) has collaborated with Communist party leaders to address the needs and problems facing the country.

China is divided into 23 provinces, including Taiwan; five autonomous regions; and the four directly administered municipalities of Beijing, Shanghai, Tianjin, and Chongqing. Although the People's Republic of China claims Taiwan as a province, Taiwan is ruled by a separate government and is outside of China's jurisdiction. These units form the first tier of China's regional government. Many provinces have existed in roughly their present geographic shape for hundreds of years.

Each province or region is divided into counties, which total more than 2,000 across the nation. These form the second tier of regional government. On average, a county may have a population from half a million to more than one million.

The smallest local government unit in rural areas is the village, and in urban areas, the district. China is beginning an effort to implement an electoral process for the selection of village and district officials.

Until recently, Hong Kong and Macau were colonies of the United Kingdom and Portugal, respectively. Hong Kong reverted to China's sovereignty on July 1, 1997, and Macau followed on December 31, 1999. These two former Western colonies are accorded special status by the Chinese government because of their different historical backgrounds and highly distinctive socioeconomic conditions. Each was made a Special Administrative Region (SAR) and is run by a government elected by the region's population. China promised not to alter the status of these two districts for 50 years after their return to China. The Chinese government offered these generous terms to try to woo people in Taiwan, in the hope of the eventual reunion of that prosperous island with mainland China.

6

China's Economy

C hina has a rapidly growing economy, which has led to sharp increases in energy demand. The transformation of the economy, over the last quarter-century, has been nothing short of a miracle. China has gained the world's attention with its recent decades of economic growth, as it assumes the role of the global factory floor for the manufacture of everything from consumer goods to major machinery.

In the 1980s, the central government reviewed the legacy of a state-run economy, and deficiencies were identified. The principle of state ownership of land was considered sacred in China. In 1992, however, the government allowed limited property speculation in urban areas. The move increased the price of land for real estate development. A mixed economy has since developed, with a combination of state-owned and private firms. The government has encouraged foreign investment, and since the 1980s, has allowed special economic zones to emerge. Now foreign investors receive preferential treatment for investing in these zones.

In the 1990s, China achieved an exceptional average annual economic growth rate of more than 11 percent. In 2007, this figure was 11.6 percent, and even in the major global recession of 2008–2009, China's growth rate stayed above 8 percent. Such economic development has affected various parts of the country differently. Urban coastal cities and their surrounding areas, particularly in the south, have experienced more accelerated economic growth than any other part of the country.

Daily life for people in Beijing or Shanghai is very different from the lives of the peasants in nearby rural provinces. Conditions for Chinese peasant farmers have not dramatically improved with the new economic direction. The gap is increasing between those who are very poor and the emerging rich. Social unrest in the poorer western provinces, the breakup of financially troubled state-owned enterprises, and the economic migration of rural people to large cities have all caused problems of unemployment and social unrest. The global economic slowdown of 2008–2009 has added to rising urban unemployment. Millions of uneducated rural migrants have flocked to Chinese cities—especially along the east coast and major rivers—in search of factory work and construction jobs. As many of these new factories face declining orders or close their doors, these recent migrants have returned home, further disrupting the demographic balance between Chinese city and countryside.

China is having a hard time blending Communist principles and capitalist business interests. Large state-owned enterprises still control much of the Chinese economy. Many are inefficient and unprofitable. An ongoing priority for the government has been to restructure some of these enterprises into private, more efficient operations.

China's growing economy has helped many of its citizens gain a higher standard of living, but there are still others, mostly in the rural farming regions, who struggle to survive. Above, investors keep track of the stock market in Hainan Province.

CHAIRMAN MAO PERIOD

For the first 30 years after the establishment of the Communist government in 1949, a series of political movements halted Chinese economic development. The Great Leap Forward and the Cultural Revolution severely damaged China's economic structure. The Great Leap Forward was Mao's idea to establish communes and to increase industrial production dramatically. Throughout the country, people were forced to make steel, even from household items, in simple backyard furnaces. The results were disastrous. The steel produced was poor quality, and agricultural production fell severely when crops were neglected. Famine resulted.

The Cultural Revolution (1966–1976) was Mao's scheme to punish his critics. Armies of young students organized into Red Guard units were encouraged to create a totally new

China. Intellectuals, teachers, and parents were all targets of humiliation, and historic buildings, museums and libraries, and books were destroyed. Students took over the universities and disrupted teaching programs, while teachers and intellectuals were sent to work on farms. It was a time of total disorder, confusion, torture, suicide, killings, and chaos throughout China.

The disruption ceased only after Mao's death in 1976. The regime of Deng Xiaoping introduced reforms. Since 1982, recovery has been remarkable. The real economic growth rate has annually exceeded the official target, which had been set at 8 percent per year.

POST-MAO ADVANCES

A key part of this economic upswing began in 1978. It was guided by Deng—who had been sent to re-education camps three times under Mao. Deng's plan was focused on renewal, development, and tentative encouragement of Western investment in China. Known as the Four Modernizations, the plan stressed new approaches for agriculture, industry, science and technology, and national defense. Thousands of students were allowed to study overseas. The new government promoted light industry, led by textile and food-processing enterprises. This was the beginning of the production of significant quantities of consumer goods in China, many of which were not made there before 1978.

The 1980s saw China make remarkable gains in industrial and agricultural production. Small-scale private enterprises were encouraged in rural and urban areas. China appeared to be on the threshold of new economic relations with other countries. In June 1989, however, the brutal suppression of student demonstrations in Tiananmen Square in Beijing caused the world to impose temporary economic sanctions on China. Tourism fell, and the economy declined. Still, economic reform continued. One year later, the United States renewed China's

most-favored-nation trading status, and other Western governments soon lifted economic sanctions.

AGRICULTURE

Farming in China started some 7,000 to 8,000 years ago. An old
Chinese saying states, "Food is the heaven of the people." Thus,
agricultural production largely focused on food crops, rather
than crops for industrial purposes or animal feed. Traditional
agricultural regions include the river valleys in central and
western China, where wheat, barley, and maize are grown; the
far south and southeast, where rice paddies dominate; and the
North China Plain, home of winter wheat. Important second-
ary crops include vegetables, melons, potatoes, sweet potatoes,
peanuts, and soybeans. In selected regions, there are apple and
pear orchards, and in the south, citrus fruits are grown. Fishponds are also important, especially in the Chang Jiang and
Pearl River lake districts. One indicator of China's achievement
is that, in 2006, its agricultural production was valued at more
than $300 billion, or more than the combined value of the agri-
cultural output of India and the United States.

SERICULTURE

The oldest and most famous traditional handicraft industry in
China is sericulture, the raising of silkworms for the production of raw silk. Even today, it is a large textile industry, second
only to cotton. Sericulture is thought to have begun as far back
as 2600 B.C. Silk was the basis for China's earliest international
trade. The most famous plantations are in the Suzhou area,
near Shanghai, and Zhejiang Province. Other noteworthy areas
are in Guangdong and Sichuan provinces. Mulberry leaves are
the preferred food of the silkworm. In the north, some silkworms feed on oak leaves, and their silk is coarser. Most of the
45,000 tons of silk produced each year are exported. China has
captured 90 percent of the world market for raw silk and 30 to
40 percent for finished silk.

For centuries, Chinese silk production has been a treasured and profitable tradition. The fabric, initially developed for the imperial family, became so popular it even inspired one of the greatest trading routes in history, the Silk Road. Above, women work with large baskets of silk cocoons in Wusih, China.

Tea

The tea plant has long been of great agricultural importance for China. Its origins trace to the second century A.D. Grown in plantations in the uplands of central China and the ranges of the coastal provinces, tea is also important in interior Sichuan Province.

Rice, Wheat, Millet, Cotton

In China, some 55 to 60 percent of the cultivated farmland is occupied by the three great food crops—rice, wheat, and millet. Rice, accounting for up to 50 percent of food production, is grown in central and south China. Wheat and millet are grown in north China.

China is the world's top producer of rice, wheat, barley, millet, and sweet potatoes. It is the second largest producer of corn, sorghum, potatoes, and soybeans. The country accounts for 15 percent of global cotton production, the most in the world. Cotton is mainly produced along the middle and lower reaches of the Huang He and Chang Jiang valleys. The southern and southeast coasts are productive areas for sugarcane, the other major non-food crop.

Animal Husbandry

Like farming, animal husbandry has a long history in China. Production of pork, beef, and mutton has reached 30 million to 35 million tons a year, placing China first in the world. One of every two pigs raised in the world is raised in China.

Fishing

Historical records note the presence of artificial fishponds in China as early as 1142 B.C. Coastal fishing dates to the eighth century B.C. Since 1950, fish production has developed rapidly, but it is a weak part of China's agriculture, amounting to less than 2 percent of the value of total agricultural production. Though there are many fish farms, the sea is the main source of fish for China.

FUTURE CHALLENGES

Agriculture in China faces serious problems. It functions at a low level of technology. The traditional emphasis is still on farming, to the exclusion of fishing, forest enterprises, and animal husbandry. Unfavorable physical conditions, such as low rainfall and temperature changes, play havoc with the stability of production. The demands of 1.34 billion people leave little room for error from year to year. Famines have occurred. The most pressing problem is the constant demand on the land caused by overuse and misuse, urban growth, and industrial expansion. Land-use planning with an emphasis on regional specialties and modern techniques is hoped to help minimize these problems.

The Chinese employment picture changed dramatically from 1950 to 2000. In 1950, agriculture accounted for 84 percent of workers, service industries 9 percent, and manufacturing 7 percent. In 2008, the figures were: agriculture 43 percent, service industries 32 percent, and manufacturing 25 percent. About half of China's workforce consists of rural workers. Most are employed in farming, forestry, fishing, and animal husbandry, or work on state-owned farms.

Agriculture has a declining share of the country's generated wealth, accounting for some 14 percent of the gross domestic product (GDP). This compares to 45 percent for industry. China's new leaders have a new perception of the country as a world economic giant—the global factory floor—with a vast potential market for foreigners. Yet agricultural production must be maintained at a meaningful level if China is to meet its future food needs. After all, the population is projected to be nearly 1.5 billion by 2025. Irrigated land, now covering more than 200,000 square miles (518,000 sq km), will also be an important part of any future agricultural picture. Nearly half of China's cultivated land is irrigated. The fear of water shortages is growing, as demands for water become greater.

INDUSTRY

In 1949, the industrial sector in China employed only one percent of the workforce. In the 1950s, as the Communist revolution swept through China, almost all industry became state-owned, and agriculture was organized into collectives. The central government directed the economy, following goals outlined in five-year plans. Industrial activity was concentrated in regions along the coast, with most industry found in former treaty ports and major river valleys. Another region of expansion was the northeast (Manchuria), where Russian and Japanese colonial interests developed heavy industries based on

local iron ore and coal resources. This early industrial development stressed heavy industries, such as iron and steel, chemicals, electric power, and textiles.

During the 1950s, much of China's industrial activity was
related to building military items. Medium-sized facilities
were based on regional self-sufficiency and the use of local
resources. Such operations were located toward the interior,
away from the more vulnerable coastline. The central government directed smaller industries to produce agricultural
equipment and building supplies. The idea was to promote
greater peasant productivity and self-sufficiency for the
communes.

MODERN DEVELOPMENT

China's industry has shown dramatic growth, especially after
Deng Xiaoping took power in 1978. By 2006, China was either
the world's leading or second-leading producer of critical lead,
zinc, tin, aluminum, cotton, raw wool, and coal. The country
brought its population explosion under control with the one-
child policy; it is improving city roads, bridges, and sewers; it
has strengthened its military; and it has become a world player.
Its trade, both regional and global, is growing.

Resources and Energy

The prosperous east coast provinces, with high-technology
industries and foreign investment, are a major part of resource
development. The central provinces emphasize energy production, heavy industry, and agricultural processing. The far
western provinces, because of their rich natural resources,
concentrate on minerals, animal grazing, and agriculture where
water is available. China's future construction projects involve
the development of a national transportation network to help
long-distance economic exchange. At the same time, the nation
is continually making efforts to diminish the widening gap
in levels of economic prosperity between the populations in

or near industrial centers and the rural populations seldom touched by the rush of coastal economic growth.

State-owned enterprises still control most commodities, including steel, coal, oil, and electric power. Prices for raw materials are kept artificially low to maximize industrial profits. In the coming years, however, the central government is expected to raise prices to better reflect the world-market level.

China is relatively rich in energy sources, particularly coal, and has expanding petroleum, natural gas, hydroelectric power, and nuclear energy. Fossil fuels provide some 82 percent of China's energy, with about three-quarters of that coming from coal. It is the largest producer and consumer of coal in the world. Oil accounts for 20 percent, followed by hydropower at 7 percent, and natural gas at 2 percent. Nuclear power is expected to generate 3 percent of electricity by 2010. That mix began to change in 2009 as the turbines in the massive Three Gorges Dam project on the Chiang Jang came into production.

Coal

China produces more than 2 billion tons of coal a year and ranks first in the world in coal production. It consumes about 25 percent of the world total and can still export coal, mainly to South Korea and Japan. Coal mines are found throughout China but are concentrated in Shanxi Province on the Loess Plateau. Another significant area is the Shanxi, Shaanxi, and Inner Mongolia borderland, which is referred to as China's "Black Triangle." Recently, large-scale open-pit mines have been established. China is increasingly open to foreign investment in the coal industry and has expressed interest in coal liquefaction technology and coal bed methane production.

Each year, 6,000 to 20,000 coal miners are killed because many coal operations are small scale and lack even basic safety controls. Explosions, underground floods, negligence, poor ventilation, and lack of safety equipment are some of the

As the world's largest consumer of coal, China burns more fuel than the combined amounts used in the United States, Europe, and Japan. Above, a coal miner in Shanxi Province carries home a sack of coal, in front of a mural of Deng Xiaopeng and Mao Zedong.

causes. Conditions are not likely to improve as China's demand for power is quickly increasing.

The burning of coal presents a major environmental problem for China. Heavy use of unwashed soft (bituminous) coal is the main source of air pollution. Sulfur dioxide and smoke dust are major pollutants. Power plants, factories, automobiles, homes, and trains also contribute. Acid rain affects up to 40 percent of the country. The World Bank recently reported that 13 of the world's 20 most air-polluted cities are in China. Further, the Chinese government has admitted that the air is polluted in more than 225 of its cities, with pollution also found in seven major watersheds.

Oil

China has made great strides in oil production. It is the fifth-largest producer in the world. Proven oil reserves for China are ranked ninth in the world, similar to the United States, with up to 24 billion barrels. China's production had grown to 3.725 million barrels per day in 2007, with annual crude oil output at 187.7 million tons that same year. It is the third largest consumer in the world, and it only became self-sufficient in 1965. This was, in part, because of a large oil field discovered in the northern Northeast China Plain. The famous Daqing field accounts for one-third of China's oil production. Other fields are in Xinjiang Autonomous Region, coastal Shandong and Liaoning provinces, and the coastal continental shelf of the Yellow, East, and South China seas.

Another dimension to the oil resource issue is China's belief that it is the rightful owner of the Spratly and the Paracel Islands, off the southeast coast in the South China Sea. China, Taiwan, the Philippines, Vietnam, and other nations have made territorial claims to the islands. The surrounding seabed is thought to have the potential for production of 1.9 million barrels a day, well over what China currently produces. China and Japan also dispute claims over parts of the East China Sea for offshore resources. In addition, national petroleum needs are escalating enormously because of the new Chinese fascination with the private automobile.

Natural Gas

Historically, natural gas has not been a major fuel in China. Traditionally, natural gas was used as a feedstock for fertilizer plants. Little was used to generate electricity. The best reserves are in the Tarim Basin in Xinjiang in western China. Domestic reserves look promising but require a huge investment for a west-to-east pipeline to service cities on the east coast. For example, in 2004, a multibillion-dollar gas pipeline, stretching 2,485 miles (4,000 km) from Shanghai to Xinjiang and perhaps into Central Asia, moved China toward a greater reliance on gas. A second west-east gas pipeline—with a length of 5,406 miles (8,700 km)—was begun in 2008, further boosting the role of natural gas in the Chinese energy equation. It is to be completed in 2011.

Other domestic gas deposits in Shanxi Province could more easily be linked to consumers in Beijing and northeast Hebei and Shandong provinces. Sichuan Province in the southwest could supply consumers in Hubei and Hunan provinces in central China. Guangdong Province uses imported liquefied natural gas for power generation. Plans call for foreign investment to help build China's first liquefied natural gas import terminal here.

Hydroelectric Energy

China, as a mountainous country, has hundreds of rivers. Yet at the time of the Communist revolution in 1949, it had only eight dams. Today, it has more than 19,000 dams. Only 20 of these dams, however, have a capacity to generate 1,000 megawatts or more of electricity. Traditionally, dams were used for irrigation and flood control. Now the country is promoting its great potential for hydroelectric power. China ranks second in the world for waterpower potential and fourth in the world in hydroelectric power produced.

The spectacular Three Gorges Dam will play a prominent role in China's near future. The 17-year project was completed in 2009, although the late addition of an underground power plant with six additional turbines will extend the construction period until 2011. The dam, the largest in the world, is on the middle Chang Jiang (Yangtze River) near Yichang in Hubei Province. It is expected to generate 84 billion kilowatt-hours of electricity a year. The reservoir is 375 miles (604 km) long, creating a lake with a water area of 32,000 square miles (83,000 sq km). This is approximately the same size as Lake Superior in the Great Lakes. The Three Gorges lake is 575 feet (175 m) deep. The wall holding the water back is 600 feet (185 m) high. The dam is expected to provide more than 10 percent of China's power needs, yet because of its immense size and the disruption of land and people, controversy has surrounded the project within and outside of China from the beginning.

More than 1,700 villages, 127 cities and towns, and 1,600 factories were submerged in the first stages of the creation of the lake behind the dam. More than 600,000 acres (242,000 hectares) of farmland have been lost. One million to two million people have been displaced, and more will still have to be moved as efforts are made to stabilize the hillsides that have been disturbed on both sides of the lake.

The creation of the dam, equipped with massive ship locks, will allow greater flood control for the river valley and give 10,000-ton ocean-going cargo ships and passenger liners direct upstream access to Chongqing. In 2004, the Three Gorges Dam—already partially operational—had to deal with the third largest autumn flood in Chinese history. The dam and its flood-control and power-generating functions all performed adequately in the face of this considerable environmental strain.

Modern industries in China are very dependent upon energy sources like hydroelectricity, coal, petroleum, and natural gas. Important parts of the economy that depend on these sources include 14 major iron and steel plants in the central and eastern parts of the country, including the largest at Anshan; chemical industries, including those that make chemical fertilizers and organic chemicals, clustered along the coastal areas; and construction-material industries of all sizes, scattered throughout the country. Engineering industries are highly diverse. They produce tools, trains, trucks, bicycles, airplanes, and machinery. Centers include numerous east coast cities and the inland cities of Wuhan, Xian, and Chongqing. Light manufacturing industries include paper and porcelain making.

Transportation

Road, rail, and air networks are important for the country. In 2009, railway lines totaled 48,364 miles (77,835 km), but only 15,181 miles (24,433 km) were electrified. The U.S. rail network, by contrast, reaches over 141,961 miles (228,464 km). China's international rail links connect with Pyongyang, North Korea; Ulan Bator, Mongolia; and Moscow, Russia. Links to Xinjiang in the far west, from the east coast, use the interior capital city of Lanzhou in Gansu Province as an east-west hub.

In 2006, a $4 billion rail extension between Lhasa in Tibet and Golmud City in Qinghai Province was completed. In developing this 720-mile (1,160-km) track, planners had to deal with permafrost and a plateau height of 3.1 miles (5 km). Oxygen is available on the train for passengers who find the thin air troubling. The north-south domestic train links include Beijing to Guangzhou and Hong Kong in the south, and Beijing to Harbin, the capital city of Heilongjiang Province in Manchuria.

In 1945, China had only 50,000 miles (80,500 km) of roads. Today, that figure exceeds 1.9 million miles (3.1 million km). Highway construction in China is rapidly proceeding. At the moment, the Beijing-Shanghai expressway is the longest in China, stretching over 700 miles (1,130 km). The country has about 25,479 miles (41,005 km) of expressways. Many four-lane highways exist in the country, usually near large cities like Beijing, Shanghai, and Guangzhou. Freeways, elevated highways, and modern bridges have been built since the early 1990s as cities expanded and modernized. Freight movement on China's roads is increasingly important. Even so, more freight is carried on inland and coastal waterways than by either rail or road.

Private car ownership has been traditionally quite limited, and bicycles still outnumber cars by at least 200 to one. Bicycles are a vital means of daily transportation everywhere. One in every three bicycles in the world is in China. There are two million privately owned cars in China, and this figure

China's most abundant resource—people—has attracted foreign investors who have poured money into the Communist country for factories and manufacturing plants. Above, an autoworker in Liaoning Province helps assemble a car for Brilliance Auto.

is quickly increasing. Western car manufacturers are targeting China. They see the potential for a vast car market, since fewer than one percent of the Chinese people owns a car. Companies and taxis account for 70 percent of car purchases. However, in 2008, China produced 9.3 million vehicles and in the first months of 2009—even with the global recession touching all countries—the Chinese purchased 3.8 million vehicles. China alone provided 25 percent of General Motors' global sales in 2009. It is thought that China may soon become the largest car market in the world. Car production in 2010 is slated for 10 million units, which would give China the second or third spot in world automobile production. In 2009, a Chinese company purchased Hummer, the large off-road vehicle, from General Motors.

Aircraft manufacture is becoming a noted industry in China. In Xian, the modern A320 plane is being built for domestic and international use. Airplanes fly more than 1,000 domestic routes, 18 regional routes, and 85 international routes. The international routes reach 60 overseas cities in 40 countries. There is large air freight demand to and from North America, Europe, parts of Southeast Asia, and Japan. Air China flies overseas, and 15 airlines, including China East, China Southern, and Dragon Air, handle domestic flights.

In recent years, the government has realized the enormous economic advantages of promoting travel within China. The economic benefits are obvious when more than one billion people are on the move within the country. The improvement of domestic air travel is a major priority, mainly using A320 planes. Other plans to increase travel include the promotion of efficient train operations, the extension of holiday time for workers, and the relentless expansion of expressways and paved roads. By 2020, it is estimated that China will be the fourth-largest source of outbound tourism in the world, sending 100 million tourists abroad.

SPECIAL ECONOMIC ZONES

The creation of special economic zones along the east coast established a significant break from a true Communist economy. As early as 1981, Shenzhen, adjacent to Hong Kong, was the first region to have greater economic freedom and favorable terms for foreign investment. Once a small, sleepy, peasant village with rice paddy cultivation, Shenzhen was transformed into a landscape with skyscrapers, a new railway station, and air links to the rest of China and beyond. Shenzhen's urban population skyrocketed—from 20,000 in 1987 to 7.5 million in 2007. This is an example of the phenomenal growth rate that some of these special economic zones achieve.

Rapid development swept the coast from Zhuhai, near Macau, north to Shantou, Xiamen, and Shanghai's Pudong district. Later, part of Hainan Island off China's far southern coast was granted special economic status. That move gave China closer access to Southeast Asia, when compared with economic rivals Japan and Taiwan.

China offers a huge domestic market, cheap plentiful labor, minimal restrictions on work conditions, and an authoritarian government. Deng Xiaoping's late 1970s government reforms set the stage. However, the effect was confined to the coast so it would cause as little disruption as possible for interior China initially. Six eastern coastal provinces, particularly Guangdong, have greatly benefited, but at the expense of other parts of China. A quarter of all of China's registered foreign enterprises are in Guangdong. Manufacturing and real estate account for more than 70 percent of all direct foreign investment. Hong Kong is by far the top investor in China. Japan, United States, and Taiwan follow.

In 1984, China decided to open up 14 east coast cities, giving preferential treatment to foreign investors. Most of the cities had once been treaty ports, with a history of foreign trade. For example, the city of Qingdao on the Shandong Peninsula has a central European atmosphere, with well-preserved old German architecture. The cities were selected based on size, links to overseas Chinese, established transport and industrial development, and the availability of local labor and talent. They stretch from Dalian city in Liaoning Province in the north to Beihai city in southern Guangxi Province.

The east coast provinces, with their special economic centers, are most favored for the promotion of high technology and consumer goods manufacturing, service sector expansion, export-oriented production, and, of course, continued foreign investment.

TRADE PATTERNS

China's more liberalized economic attitude has had an impact on the country's trade patterns. Ten years ago, China was fifteenth among the largest trading nations in the world. Now, including Hong Kong, it is ranked third. Trade is vital to China's future economic development.

The United States is China's largest trading partner (2008) at $409.2 billion. Imports from the United States amounted to $71.5 billion, and exports to the United States were $337.7 billion. Japan was second at $266.4 billion in trade with $124.2 billion in imports and $142.2 billion in exports. Third was Hong Kong at $87.4 billion. China treats Hong Kong as a separate trading partner. South Korea, Germany, and Taiwan are China's other major trading partners. International trade for China rose from approximately $475 billion in 2000 to more than $900 billion in 2006. The country is second to the United States as the world's leading recipient of direct foreign investment.

Manufactured goods account for 85 percent of China's trade. Exports include manufactured goods, clothing, footwear, electrical appliances, telecommunications equipment, transport equipment, and food and livestock products. China has become the chief supplier of low-cost consumer goods to the United States. Imports include machinery and transport equipment, basic goods, chemicals, and crude materials.

China is the fastest-growing export market for the United States. The trade balance with the United States skews heavily in China's favor. The Chinese government is continually trying to make concessions to prevent this imbalance from getting worse. Trade with the United States is never simple. It may be influenced by long-standing issues, such as human-rights abuses, theft of nuclear information, military weapons and build-up, and the status of Taiwan. In 2000, China concluded a comprehensive trade agreement with the United States, which paved the way for China's entry into the World Trade Organization in 2001. China agreed to open most sectors of its economy to increased foreign participation, allowing concessions in the energy sector.

China is fast becoming the hungry dragon. In terms of imports, the capacity—both actual and potential—for consumption is monumental. In terms of global trade, China is the world's largest consumer of rice, lead, zinc, tin, nickel, aluminum, rubber, raw wool, cotton, major oil seeds, and coal. It is the second largest consumer of wheat, coarse grains, tea, and oil. With the size of the Chinese population, its growing adoption of consumerism, and the country's 8 to 11 percent annual economic growth rate, the potential exists for major tensions in that capacity to consume.

MONETARY POLICY

The exchange rate for China's official currency, the yuan, was allowed to float on the international money market in 1992. At the time, one U.S. dollar was worth five yuan. The exchange rate became one U.S. dollar to eight yuan in 1997, and the rate has remained constant since then.

CURRENT CHALLENGES

Environmental problems continue to impact the country. Rapid industrialization and economic expansion, the unprecedented growth of Chinese cities, and a heavy reliance on the burning of coal contribute greatly to the severity of the problem. Air, water, and soil—the basic components of the environment—fare badly in China. In preparation for the 2008 Olympic Games, China enacted strict driving and manufacturing calendars so that air pollution might be kept at a minimum.

In a ranking of the 38 most polluted cities globally, China has 23. This is one world-ranking list that China has no interest in making. Yet, with coal being a source for more than 75 percent of China's power generation and the addition of thousands of cars to the streets of China each week, this environmental problem is likely to plague the country for some time to come.

Rapid economic growth in China poses another serious problem. The demand for electricity is expected to double over the next 15 years. Now everyone wants a television and an air conditioner. As coal-fired plants emit pollution into the air, China's consumption of coal is projected to double by 2020. Skyrocketing demand for electricity could bring brownouts and blackouts. China's economic engine also could face serious interruptions.

One problem that accompanied China's new economic reforms in recent years was an increase in official corruption. A get-rich-quick attitude developed at all levels, both in the government and in the private sector.

Another concern over rapid economic development in China has been the creation of regional disparities. The United Nations China National Human Development Reports ranked all provinces, autonomous regions, and municipalities, based on an index that factored in lifespan, education, and income. Shanghai, Beijing, and other coastal areas such as Tianjin, Guangdong, Liaoning, Zhejiang, Jiangsu, and Fujian ranked high, first through eighth. Other coastal areas ranked moderately high, including Hainan Island. At the bottom of the scale, ranked twenty-fifth to thirty-first, were Sichuan, Ningxia, Yunnan, Gansu, Qinghai, Guizhou, and Tibet. The crux of the regional disparities relate to the critical and growing gap in income between the poor in rural China and the urban populations. The forces of economic growth have been centered in the cities, particularly on the east coast, and in relatively wealthy rural villages that have picked up some of the development traits of urban populations.

When China, in its entirety, is compared to the outside world, using the 2008 United Nations Human Development index, it ranked 94th out of 179 countries. Norway was first, Japan was eighth, the United States was fifteenth, and Hong Kong was twenty-third.

If such trends continue, it is likely that regional differences in the quality of life will only magnify in the coming years. Government mechanisms are necessary to redistribute the prosperity of the eastern coastal provinces and to filter future development increasingly to the central and western provinces.

7

Regional Contrasts

G eography has always been a subject of interest for Chinese scholars. A classic book written in the fifth century B.C. divided China into nine regions. For each region, an inventory detailed mountains, rivers, lakes, swamps, soils, and chief economic products. A later book, written in the third century B.C., divided land into first- and second-level types based on physical characteristics, such as hills, soils, and surface materials. Many of these early books were regional geography studies of the provinces and counties. Chinese scholars have completed more than 9,000 regional studies.

The Chinese Academy of Science has compiled separate 8- and 12-volume works that classify China into regions, using physical characteristics and land types. One can divide China into six easily identifiable regions: Northeast, North China Plain, Chang Jiang

Drainage Area, Subtropical South China, Inner Mongolia-Xin-jiang Steppe lands, and the Tibetan Plateau.

NORTHEAST

The northeast, also known as Manchuria, encompasses the three provinces of Liaoning, Jilin, and Heilongjiang. It is considered a peripheral part of the country because of its harsh winter climate, its isolation, and before 1900, its sparse settlement. The region is rich in natural resources, such as coal and iron ore, but quite limited in agricultural land. People from this region ruled China for the last 300 years of its imperial history during the Qing Dynasty. In the recent past, it has been coveted and occupied by Russia and Japan. With an area of 408,880 square miles (1,059,000 sq km) and a population of 108 million, the northeast will continue to be vital to China. Of particular importance is its proximity to Siberia, North Korea, and Japan, as well as the Yellow Sea.

In the 1950s, the Communist government devoted considerable attention to this part of the country. The discovery of oil at Daqing—50 miles (80 km) northwest of Harbin, the capital city of Heilongjiang province—enabled China to open its largest oil field. The heavy industrial character of the area is evident in Anshan city, in Liaoning Province, which produces 20 percent of China's steel. Dalian, at the southern tip of the Liaodong Peninsula, is the only important port in the northeast. The maritime climate makes this deep-water port ice-free. An extensive rail network helped in the development of this region as well. The Russians built part of the Manchurian railway through Harbin, linking Siberia to their far eastern naval port of Vladivostok.

Historically, the region was referred to as a great northern wilderness, with considerable mountain forest and open plains. Farming was introduced in the third century A.D. The Manchus, the indigenous people of Manchuria, developed an economy based on hunting and fishing. Gradually, the region became China's northern granary. During the Qing Dynasty, Chinese were not allowed to settle in Dongbei, as the northeast region was also called, because it was the Manchu homeland and they wanted to keep it as a fallback region if the Qing lost control of China. The dynasty fell in 1911, and by the middle of the twentieth century, Dongbei had become an important migrant destination, especially as the iron and steel industry grew around Anshan and Shenyang in Liaoning Province.

NORTH CHINA PLAIN

No region is more important to China than the Huang He (Yellow River) basin, which forms part of the strategic North China Plain. This is an area of more than 386,100 square miles (one million sq km), with a population of more than 350 million. It includes Beijing and Tianjin on the northern margin, and the provinces of Hebei, Shandong, Shanxi, Henan, Shaanxi, and Ningxia, and parts of Gansu province in the west-central part of the basin. The Qin Ling Mountains and the Huai River define the southern boundary of this region. The Huang He (Yellow River) watershed is identified as the cradle of Chinese civilization. It has supported an agricultural society for more than 7,000 years, longer than any other place on Earth. Beijing, as the present capital, is the home to administrative and architectural masterpieces, unsurpassed in the rest of the country.

This region has seen its share of erosion and devastating floods and earthquakes. Some people say that this part of China has the longest continuous history of vulnerability. The channel and waters of the Huang He shaped and molded the region. In the last 2,000 years, the river has changed its course about 10 times and flooded some 1,500 times. The river, as it winds its way through Gansu, Shaanxi, and Shanxi provinces, picks up the characteristic loess soil and displays the distinctive yellowish color for hundreds of miles until it finally flows into the Gulf of Bohai and the Yellow Sea. Heavy silting has raised the riverbed so that when a dike does break and the river floods, there is nowhere for the water to re-enter the river, making it easier to understand why the Huang He is also called "China's Sorrow." Since silting, erratic water flow, and shifting shoals make navigation difficult, the Huang He has never functioned as a major river highway. Its use has been confined to local fishing, short trips, and local ferry and barge traffic.

Shandong Province, with the capital of Jinan and the seaport of Qingdao, encompasses an open fertile plain through which the Huang He completes its journey to the sea. For centuries, the province was considered one of China's poorer regions. Yet the fertility of the soil meant that human settlement here was continuous for more than 6,000 years. Qufu, located 100 miles (160 km) directly south of Jinan, is the birthplace and burial site of Confucius. A thriving tourist trade promoting sites like Qufu and the former German port of Qingdao has revived the province's economy. Just south of Jinan is the holiest of China's five sacred mountains, Taishan. A 5,070-foot (1,545-m) climb leads to the summit, which is one of Taoism's holiest places. This major pilgrimage site also honors Buddhism and Confucianism. The Chinese people have probably worshipped at this site longer than they have had written history.

The famous Loess Plateau in the western part of the region is considered the ancient heartland of China. The loess deposits that cover the plateau are 200 feet (61 m) deep, on average. Extensive erosion of the plateau and severe soil loss have plagued this area. Each year, up to 2 billion tons of soil wash into the river, and three-quarters of that reaches the Yellow Sea. Traditionally, the Loess Plateau was a link connecting central China to the western part of the country via the Silk Road. Modern-day Xian, in the southwestern part of the plateau, is home to the famous Terracotta Warriors. This ancient city has a distinctive perimeter wall that forms a rectangle whose sides total 8 miles (12 km) in length.

One of China's most famous natural features is the Loess Plateau. Located in the western region of the North China Plain, residents of the plateau have lived for centuries in distinctive, cave-like houses carved out of the sides of the mountains. Above, hills on the Loess Plateau featuring the region's unique shelters.

The North China Plain is the largest and most populous expanse of flat, cultivated land in China. Villages appear at regular intervals, and rows of trees mark fields and farms on the flat terrain. Diked canals appear in all directions. These are part of an ancient irrigation system, as well as an attempt to control the unpredictable Huang He.

The same geographical conditions that helped make this area historically important for agriculture and settlement have also helped make it a prime focus of highway construction. As the Chinese increasingly turn to automobile travel, highway links weave all across the North China Plain, tying together Beijing, China's main tourist destination, and cities along the coast and on the Shandong peninsula, as well as the Great Wall and Xian with its Terracotta Warriors.

Some researchers describe the North China Plain as an excellent example of a core area. It contains the capital and other major cities, including Tianjin, a seaport and major industrial complex on the Bohai Gulf. In addition, the North China Plain is one of the most densely populated and highly productive agricultural areas in all of China.

CHANG JIANG DRAINAGE AREA

Unlike the continuous, flat, agricultural, and urban-industrial land associated with the sediment-laden Huang He to the north, the basins and valleys of the Chang Jiang Drainage Area display variations in relief and elevation. The Chang Jiang begins its very long journey across the country in the mountains of northern Tibet. Some 700 tributaries contribute to its flow. Large cities have developed along its route—Chongqing, Wuhan, and Nanjing. Near its mouth lies Shanghai, which came into prominence in the nineteenth century as a banking, trading, and shipping center. It was the Chinese base for European imperialism. The river valley itself is estimated to occupy about one-fifth of China's land area and one-fourth of its total farmland, and it holds approximately one-third of China's population. Seventy percent of China's rice production and 40 percent of its total food production come from the Chang Jiang Basin. The middle and lower portion of the river is one of the largest and busiest inland waterways in the world. The completion of the Three Gorges Dam now makes the area less susceptible to annual floods.

The Grand Canal, the world's largest manmade waterway, dates back to its beginnings in 600 B.C. The canal linked the delta area of the Chang Jiang with the Huang He and Beijing to the north. The idea was to provide an easy route to transport surplus rice from the lower Chang Jiang Basin to the populated parts of the north. Before the canal, the journey could take three months by barge.

Two important cities linked to the Grand Canal are Hangzhou and Nanjing. Hangzhou is the southern terminus, renowned for its silk and the scenic beauty of its famous West Lake. Marco Polo described Hangzhou near the end of the thirteenth century as the "City of Heaven." It was reported to be Mao's favorite retreat, and it was where he entertained U.S. President Richard Nixon in 1972.

Nanjing, the capital of Jiangsu Province, lies on the south bank of the Chang Jiang. It has been a capital at various times during the last 2,000 years. Sun Yat-sen's impressive cobalt blue mausoleum is located in a beautiful park on the eastern edge of the city. One of the worst atrocities of World War II happened in Nanjing, where Japanese soldiers slaughtered more than 300,000 civilians from 1937 to 1945.

Nanjing was walled as early as 2,500 years ago. Its city wall, 20 miles (32 km) long, is the longest city wall in the world. Its three-mile-long (five-km) Yangtze River bridge is a source of Chinese engineering pride. Opened in 1968, the bridge was the first major structure built solely by the Chinese after they split with the Soviets in 1960. The double-decker bridge allows for train and vehicle crossings.

Upstream along the Chang Jiang, there is always an unending parade of large and small vessels, including "large trains" of six or more barges pushed by a tug. The Chang Jiang is one of the busiest waterways in the world and is the leading transit corridor for inland China.

The middle part of the Chang Jiang, south and east of Wuhan city, has a unique physical feature. This is China's best-known and most extensive freshwater lake district, which includes an internationally recognized wetland zone. This series of rivers and lakes is essentially a network of small, shallow freshwater lakes and marshes fed by a multitude of rivers. Most are located in Hunan and Jiangxi provinces. The river network is quite dense, with many tributary systems. Between 2,500 and 3,000 river systems can be identified. Alluvial plain development has allowed for great agricultural production, especially rice. Over the centuries, the lake district has acted as a reservoir for the floodwaters of the Chang Jiang in summer. When the floodwaters come, the lake district can reach 1,350 square miles (3,500 sq km), with the deepest point only 98 feet (30 m). When the waters recede, the exposed land can support livestock and agriculture. The Three Gorges Dam has already begun to modify this annual flux in lake levels in the region.

Sichuan, through which the Chang Jiang passes, is one of China's most populous provinces. It is divided into two distinct parts: a densely populated eastern plain and a mountainous west. The productive eastern section is the fertile Red Basin, named for its underlying red sandstone. The basin has been intensively cultivated for more than 2,000 years, and several kingdoms were founded here. It is said to contain the largest concentrated rice paddy cultivation network in the world.

Chengdu, the capital city of Sichuan, is 250 miles (400 km) north of Xichang, the launch site for China's space program. Communications satellites have been launched from the Space Flight Center, with varying degrees of success. In 1996, some 500 villagers were killed when a heavy carrier rocket crashed to Earth 22 seconds after launch, leading to the development of a new satellite launch center on Hainan Island. It is slated to be completed in 2013.

SUBTROPICAL SOUTH CHINA

This region takes in the area south of the Chang Jiang, including the provinces of Fujian, Yunnan, Guangdong, and Hainan Island and the Guangxi Autonomous Region. It also includes parts of Hunan, Jiangxi, and Zhejiang provinces, as well as the cities of

Hong Kong and Macau. Since the seventeenth century, merchant classes have prospered in this subtropical coastal environment. The entrepreneurial spirit emerged early and became very much a southern characteristic. Over time, the south thought of itself as separate from the rest of China, as demonstrated by the colonial enclaves of Hong Kong and Macau.

This region of China can be very green and lush, with a wet, steamy climate. It has rolling hills dotted with cultivated terraces for agriculture. Summers are hot, winters are mild, and rainfall is spread evenly throughout the year. Yet typhoons can plague this part of China. Rice and water buffalo are seen everywhere even though some mechanized farming is now evident. Architecture is distinctive with two-story houses and an absence of walled courtyards. The indented coastline with its excellent harbors has fostered a fishing culture and continuous foreign contact and trade dating back to the Tang Dynasty (A.D. 618–907).

Traditionally, the southeast coast of China has been a window to the outside world. Hong Kong and Macau have long been ports for this part of China. The Xi (West) River, China's southernmost river, forms a strategic delta area accompanying the Pearl River as both enter the South China Sea. The delta is home to China's two rapidly expanding economic complexes— Guangzhou (Canton) and Shenzhen, a special economic zone and one of the fastest-growing cities in the world.

Hong Kong is located on an irregularly shaped peninsula and a number of offshore islands east of the Pearl River delta. The city, once a cluster of small villages, is now a modern landscape with stylistic architecture and massive towering buildings that hug steep slopes. An ultra-modern subway system connects the city to a new airport.

Forty miles (64 km) from Hong Kong, Macau occupies the tip of a peninsula and a couple of offshore islands. It has evolved into a large casino playground. Its wealth can be seen in high-rise hotels, bridges, highways, and a newly expanded airport. Its Portuguese colonial past predates Hong Kong's by 300 years.

Guangzhou (Canton), capital of the province of Guang-dong and a city of 9 million people, is another vital component of this southeast region. Open to foreigners longer than any other city in China, it attracted traders from as far away as central Asia and the Middle East. Guangdong is perhaps the most prosperous province in all of China. Located just south of the Tropic of Cancer, it has no real winter. The area grows two crops of rice and one vegetable crop a year, as well as plenty of fruit. It, too, has prospered greatly from being a major tourist destination.

Even though Guangzhou has long been the most important trading center in South China, the entire area has become an economic powerhouse. Today, there are five other trading and manufacturing centers along this south coast: Xiamen in Fujian Province; Shantou in eastern Guangdong Province; Shenzhen, adjacent to booming Hong Kong; Zhuhai across from Macau; and Haikou, on Hainan Island off Leizhou Peninsula.

The other distinctive part of subtropical China is the Yun-nan-Guizhou Plateau. Noted for its natural beauty, the plateau is a rough, mountainous land. Yunnan Province is one of the most heavily forested regions in China. It is home to many of China's native plant species and one-third of the country's 400 bird species. It has been called China's "National Botani-cal Garden." The average elevation is 3,300 feet (1,005 m). The region, which has a warm and mild climate, the most pleasant in China, is described as "spring at all seasons." It has rich agri-culture with the cultivation of rice, winter wheat, tea, hemp, and beans. On the Vietnam-Laos border, the climate becomes hotter and wetter, ideal for growing rubber trees and sugarcane, as well as bananas and other tropical fruits and vegetables.

The region's outstanding natural wonder is Shilin, the Stone Forest, south of the capital city, Kunming. It is a 300-million-year-old exposed and extensive karst (limestone) formation of rocks weathered into unusual shapes. From a distance, the gray rocky outcrops resemble a petrified forest.

Half of China's 55 minority peoples live in Yunnan. The Guangxi-Zhuang Autonomous Region is home to the largest minority group, the Zhuang, with 20 million people. In contrast, the largest ethnic group, the Han, number more than 1.25 billion people.

The border areas between Sichuan, Yunnan, and Guizhou provinces are home to the Yi people, another large ethnic minority group. They number some 7 million people. Most of the Yi live in the mountainous areas, and for hundreds of years, they were isolated farmers. Thus, their language and shamanistic religion are unique in China. In shamanism, certain people are considered spiritually gifted, believed to possess the power to access good and evil spirits. In the past decade, this region has experienced new commerce from tourism. Because of its isolation and minority culture, Dali, south of Kunming and near the terminus of the old Silk Road, has become a popular destination, particularly with people described as "hippies."

INNER MONGOLIA-XINJIANG STEPPE LANDS

This vast and remote area, lying beyond the Great Wall and long considered a peripheral part of China. accounts for one-third of the country's land area. For the Chinese, the region is considered isolated, subject to the weather extremes, and occupied by "barbarians." This vast area of steppe and grassland, desert and mountain plateau, is home to significant minority peoples, such as Mongols, Uighurs, and Kazakhs. As such, the various sections are not considered provinces, but autonomous regions. The 6 million people of the Mongolian Steppe lands and the 9 million Muslim Uighur people of the Xinjiang Autonomous Region of the northwest have been reluctant subjects of Chinese rule. Both areas have, since the eighteenth century, been brought under tight Chinese control.

China values this region primarily for its mineral resources. It is the richest in the country for rare minerals. At least 60 verifiable mineral ores are dispersed over 500 locations. Included are such standards as coal and iron, but also there are chromium, uranium, lead, zinc, gold, and salt.

The Xinjiang Autonomous Region is considered the least hospitable place in all of China, covered by arid deserts and mountains. Its two giant basins are surrounded on all sides by mountains. To the north is the grassland Jungar Basin and to the south is the Tarim Basin, dominated by the hot and dry Taklamakan Desert. The region is more than 1,865 miles (3,000 km) from any coast. Xinjiang is usually associated with the Uighur people. Other minority people, such as the Kazakhs and Kyrgyz, have cultural connections with the people across the border in the five republics of former Soviet Central Asia. A curious feature of this region is that the sun rises around 9:00 or 10:00 A.M. in the morning and sets at midnight. This is because China uses only one time zone, Beijing time.

Turfan, largely populated by Uighurs, is a fertile oasis situated in the Tian Shan. It is 505 feet (154 m) below sea level, making it the second lowest point on the planet. Only the shore of the Dead Sea, located between Jordan and Israel, is lower. Depressions such as these are a characteristic feature of this northern part of western China. Land temperatures can reach 104°F (40°C), with rainfall of only an inch or two (2.5 to 5 centimeters) a year. Famous for its grapes, Turfan, called the "City of Grapes," is also known as the "hottest, lowest, driest, and sweetest" spot in China. It is also noted for its underground water channel, known as *karez*, or *qanat*. This is a system of shafts and irrigation channels that capture snow and melt water from nearby mountains to be used in the otherwise arid basin. This underground water management system, which is more than 2,000 years old, prevents evaporation of water in the intense summer heat.

This remote region has extensive reserves of coal, oil, and natural gas. Experiments in space technology, rocketry, and sophisticated weaponry are also conducted here, far away from foreign observers. Because of the region's isolation, the government once sent notorious criminals and political opponents to prison camps here.

Urumqi, the capital, is home to more than 2 million people. It is an important transportation hub and was a strategic mountain pass route on the old Silk Road. Thirteen minority nationalities, including Huis, Uighurs, Manchus, and Mongols, inhabit Urumqi. The city is so vital to China as the most westerly industrial outpost that, in 1992, it was officially declared a "port." Thus, the city received special low tax rates and other privileges usually permitted only in port cities like Shanghai and Shantou, near Guangdong.

China's most westerly city is Kashgar, with a population of 300,000. It is located at 76°E longitude. It is more than 2,485 miles (4,000 km) from Beijing. This oasis city is the point at which the north and south arms of the Silk Road joined to form China's "front door," or natural gateway, through the Pamir mountain passes to Russia and India. Russian and British diplomats and spies converged here in the late 1800s to collect information on one another's activities. Today, it displays one of the few remaining towering outdoor statues of Chairman Mao.

TIBETAN PLATEAU

The "Roof of the World," called Xizang by the Chinese, is Tibet. The massive Tibetan Plateau, with an average elevation of 14,765 feet (4,500 m), is surrounded on all sides by towering mountain ranges. It is the source for at least five of the major rivers of east and south Asia. Some of the most spectacular scenery in the world is in this region of China, and human settlements appear to be dwarfed by high mountains. The Tibetan Plateau has an area of 965,255 square miles (2.5 million sq km),

In 2003, China became the third country in history, after the United States and Russia, to launch a human into space. Since then, scientists and engineers in China's space program have been working on a rocket that will transport their astronauts to the moon for lunar exploration. Above, a weather satellite is launched in Shanxi Province.

about one-fourth of China's total land area. This is the largest, highest, and geologically youngest plateau in the world. It contains the largest and has the most numerous lakes in China.

Tibet is the one place where Chinese troops have imposed harsh rule on the population and, in the process, forced the political and spiritual leader, the fourteenth Dalai Lama, to flee the country. Since the early 1950s, the Chinese have encouraged

Han migrations into Lhasa, the Tibetan capital region, and along the India border. The Chinese administer Xizang as an autonomous region.

Distinctive Tibetan Buddhist culture began in the eighth century and was flourishing by the eleventh century. The traditional economy is based on raising and grazing animals, including sheep, goats, horses, and cattle. It is the yak, a draft animal, however, that best symbolizes the culture of this area. The yak provides meat, milk, cheese, butter, hide, fur, hair, and butterfat, and its dung is used for fuel.

Unique in this region of China is the great variation in temperature. Diurnal range, the difference between daytime and nighttime temperatures, can reach 82°F (28°C). July temperatures in Tibet are the lowest in China, at 50°F (10°C).

Despite decades of Chinese control, and the sometimes brutal repression inflicted on Tibet, the area's traditions continue, the Buddhist monasteries still function, and the beauty of the landscape remains. The new Lhasa-Golmud railway, with its connections to south and eastern China, has generated a new tourist flow into Tibet. Such traffic has, as is always the case, introduced not just new economic growth but also changing cultural influences on the once-isolated roof of the world.

CHAPTER

8

China Looks Ahead

The twentieth century saw dynamic forces change China's political landscape. Shortly after the century began, the ages-old imperial dynastic system was swept away. By mid-century, China was ruled by a Communist system under the authoritarian Chairman Mao Zedong. By century's end, China was challenging global realities by its effective experiment with forms of capitalism. Along the way, the country survived occupation by foreign troops, a short-lived republican government, a failed attempt at monarchical restoration, a war against Japan, and years of civil war.

The People's Republic of China emerged on October 1, 1949. The past 60 years have seen major land and social reform, the Great Leap Forward campaign, famine, the Cultural Revolution, the market reforms of Deng Xiaoping, and the move to capture, for China, major positions on the world political and economic map. Through it all, Chinese civilization has endured and even thrived. Its rich history and cultural heritage have equipped its people well to forge ahead. There is a strong sense of unity that has held the Chinese nation together for more than 4,000 years. Its stable territorial boundaries, borders that defy easy penetration, and culture (including its distinctive languages, rich philosophy, and political institutions) have allowed China to remain unified through dynastic changes and periodic social upheavals. The country has been resilient and enduring. Even with regional and, occasionally, local forces calling for change, China has proven itself ready to proclaim this century as "The Chinese Century."

Decades of reform have created many vested interests, both collective and private, in the growth of the Chinese economy. Such growth is now linked to the global economy. China is a huge country with enormous resources, both natural and human, and it has much untapped potential. There are vast reserves of coal and modest confirmed reserves of petroleum. The Three Gorges Dam symbolizes the country's massive hydroelectric potential as well as its engineering capabilities. Some observers feel that China may well have the world's largest economy within just a few decades. Yet, this booming economy brings with it the likelihood of ongoing environmental degradation. Even today, as air and water quality are deteriorating, the Chinese are pouring major resources into solutions for such environmental problems. For China, the unprecedented threat for future survival comes not from outside but from landscape elements within. There is critical need to determine the best way to balance continued economic development, global outreach, and effective environmental management.

Three million soldiers and 1.2 million reserves help exert internal control over China's changing society. The military will continue to play an integral role in the twenty-first century. On paper, the country has the largest standing military

Above, a man flies a kite commemorating World AIDS Day in front of the National Olympic Stadium in Beijing. In 2008, China successfully hosted the Olympic Games, but continues to fall short in other areas, such as reporting HIV/AIDS cases. Although China has come a long way, many question if it can continue to adjust to the growing demands of the population and environmental changes.

in the world, but it has an antiquated arsenal and relatively poorly equipped troops. However, it does have atomic weapons and nuclear technology. It is developing a navy. It continues to enhance its foreign intelligence-gathering capabilities. In the first half of the 1990s, China was the sixth-largest arms exporter and seventh-largest arms importer in the world. Western powers will continue to watch the Chinese military.

The status of Taiwan touches a raw nerve in Beijing, since the Chinese regard the island as a traditional province of China. The future of relations between China and Taiwan remains uncertain. The two systems may be able to coexist for some time, with occasional disagreements, as the two economies become ever more intertwined. Recent modifications in travel restrictions between China and Taiwan are evidence of this coexistence.

As in the past, China's economy will continue to rely on agriculture in the immediate future. Food production must keep pace with the increase in population. The one-child policy has played an enormous role in bringing population growth under control. The projected population change for China between 2001 and 2050 is 8 percent, compared with 58 percent in India, where similar birth-control measures have not been implemented. A generation ago, Deng Xiaoping introduced the idea that "it is glorious to be rich." If such riches are not distributed more evenly among its people, China could face serious internal problems. As an example of its innovative search for new strategies, China has become an active participant in BRIC, an economic alliance among Brazil, Russia, India, and China. These four "emerging nations" see themselves as possibly developing stronger economies than today's Group of 8 countries (a forum for the governments of the eight richest countries) in a matter of decades—or sooner. China wants to be ready to be both a player and a leader in this evolution of global economic development.

Over the centuries, the Chinese have always had a strong attachment to the land. Family and land were the cornerstones on which Chinese society was founded. Increasing personal mobility and the trend toward a technological-industrial society rather than an agrarian one could unravel the traditional Chinese social fabric. China has grown from 20 percent urban in the 1950s to nearly 50 percent urban today. The traditional role of agriculture is threatened now, as people "vote with their feet" and move to the city. China's recently gained title as the "world's factory floor" has demographic, economic, social, and political implications.

While China's past has been one of slow and steady adaptation to change, its future will be characterized by a more rapid and profound adjustment to demographic, economic, political, environmental, and cultural transformation. It is perhaps within this strategy of careful evaluation of foreign influences that governed the nation's past greatness that China's best approach to an uncertain future lies.

Facts at a Glance

NOTE: All data 2009 unless otherwise indicated

Physical Geography

Location	Eastern Asia, bordering the Korea Bay, Bohai Gulf, Yellow Sea, East China Sea, Taiwan Strait, the South China Sea, and the Gulf of Tonkin, between Hainan Island and North Vietnam
Area	3.7 million square miles (9.6 million sq km)
Land Boundaries	Border Countries: North Korea, 880 miles (1,416 km); Russia (northeast), 2,240 miles (3,605 km); Mongolia, 2,905 miles (4,677 km); Russia (northwest), 25 miles (40 km); Kazakhstan, 950 miles (1,533 km); Kyrgyzstan, 530 miles (858 km), Tajikistan, 260 miles (414 km); Afghanistan, 45 miles (76 km); Pakistan, 325 miles (523 km); India, 2,100 miles (3,380 km); Nepal, 770 miles (1,236 km); Bhutan, 290 miles (470 km); Burma, 1,360 miles (2,185 km); Laos, 260 miles (423 km); Vietnam 795 miles (1,281 km)
Climate	Extremely diverse; tropical in the south to cold subarctic in the north; eastern coast dominated by seasonal reversal of winds called the Asiatic monsoon
Terrain	Plains, deltas, hills in the east; mountains, high plateaus, deserts in the west
Elevation Extremes	Lowest Point: Turfan Depression, -505 feet (-154 m) Highest Point: Mount Everest (Qomolangma), 29,035 feet (8,850 m)
Land Use	Arable land, 14.86%; permanent crops, 1.27%; other, 83.87% (2005)
Irrigated Land	210,976 square miles (545,960 sq km) (2003)
Natural Hazards	Frequent typhoons (hurricanes)—up to seven per year along the southern and eastern coasts; floods, earthquakes, droughts, infrequent tsunamis
Environmental Issues	Air pollution (greenhouse gases, sulfur dioxide particulates) from heavy use of coal, which produces acid rain; rapidly increasing use of automobiles causing smog pollution; water shortages, particularly in the north; water pollution from untreated wastes; deforestation; soil erosion; desertification; loss of plant and animal species

Environment

International Agreements Party to: Antarctic-Environmental Protocol, Antarctic Treaty, Biodiversity, Climate Change, Climate Change-Kyoto Protocol, Desertification, Endangered Species, Environmental Modification, Hazardous Wastes, Law of the Sea, Marine Dumping, Ozone Layer Protection, Ship Pollution, Tropical Timber 83, Tropical Timber 94, Wetlands, Whaling. Signed, but not ratified: none of the selected agreements

Population & Culture

Population 1,338,612,968; males, 688,376,749; females, 650,236,219

Population Growth Rate 0.655%

Net Migration Rate -0.39 migrants per 1,000 population

Fertility Rate 1.79 children born/woman

Birth Rate 14 children born/1,000 population

Death Rate 7.06 deaths/1,000 population

Life Expectancy at Birth Total population: 73.47 years; male, 71.61 years; female, 75.52 years

Median Age Total: 34.1 years; male, 33.5 years; female, 34.7 years

HIV/AIDS-Adult Prevalence Rate 0.1% (2007 estimate)

People Living with HIV/AIDS 700,000 (2007 est)

HIV/AIDS Deaths 39,000 (2007 est)

Ethnic Groups Han Chinese 91.5%; others 8.5%, including Zhuang, Manchu, Miao, Hui, Uighur, Yi, Tujia, Tibetan, Mongol, Buyi, Dong, Yao, and Korean (2000 census)

Religions Officially atheist, but the People's Republic of China recognizes four religions: 6% Buddhist, 2% Taoist, 2% Muslim, 1% Christian

Languages Standard Chinese or Mandarin (Putonghua, based on Beijing dialect), Yue (Cantonese), Wu (Shanghainese), Minbei (Fuzhou), Minnan (Hokkien-Taiwanese), Xiang, Gan, Hakka dialects, minority languages

Literacy (Age 15 and over who can read and write) Total population: 90.9%; male, 95.1%; female, 86.5% (2000 census)

Facts at a Glance

Economy

Currency	Renminbi yuan (RMB)
	NOTE: data are in 2008 U.S. dollars
GDP Purchasing Power Parity (PPP)	$7.973 trillion (2008 est)
	$7.315 trillion (2007 est)
	$6.473 trillion (2006 est)
GDP Per Capita	$6,000 (2008 est)
	$5,500 (2007 est)
	$4,900 (2006 est)
Labor Force	807.3 million (2008 est)
Labor Force by Occupation	Agriculture, 43%; industry, 25%; services, 32% (2006 est)
Unemployment	4% (2008 est)
	NOTE: Official data for urban areas only; including rural areas may boost total unemployment to 9%
Agricultural Products	Rice, wheat, potatoes, corn, peanuts, tea, millet, barley, apples, cotton, oilseed, pork, fish
Industries	Mining and ore processing, iron, steel, aluminum, and other metals, coal; machine building; armaments; textiles and apparel; petroleum; cement; chemicals; fertilizers; consumer products, including footwear, toys, and electronics; food processing; transportation equipment, including automobiles, rail cars and locomotives, ships, and aircraft; telecommunications equipment, commercial space launch vehicles, satellites
Exports	$1.435 trillion (2008 est)
Imports	$1.074 trillion (2008 est)
Leading Trade Partners	Exports: United States 18.6%, Hong Kong 12.7%, Japan 8.2%, South Korea 5.1%, Germany 4.2 (2008); Imports: Japan 12.2%, South Korea 10%, United States 6.6%, Hong Kong 4.9%, Germany 4.5% (2008)
Exports Commodities	Electrical and other machinery, including data-processing equipment, apparel, textiles, iron and steel, optical and medical equipment
Imports Commodities	Electrical and other machinery, oil and mineral fuels, optical and medical equipment, metal ores, plastics, organic chemicals
Transportation	Roadways: 1,199,584 miles (1,930,543 km), 979,014 miles (1,575,571 km) paved, including 25,479 miles

(41,005 km) of expressway; railways: 48,364 miles (77,835 km), 15,181 miles (24,433 km) electrified; airports: 425 with paved runways, 57 with unpaved runways; waterways: 68,350 miles (110,000 km)

Ports and Terminals Dalian, Guangzhou, Ningbo, Qingdao, Qinhuangdao, Shanghai, Shenzhen, Tianjin

Government

Country Name Conventional long form: People's Republic of China; conventional short form: China

Capital City Beijing

Type of Government Communist

Chief of State President Hu Jintao

Head of Government Premier Wen Jiabao

Independence 221 B.C. (unified under Qin Dynasty)
Qing Dynasty replaced by republic on February 12, 1912.
People's Republic of China established October 1, 1949

Communications

TV Stations 3,240 (1997)

Radio Stations 628 (AM, 369; FM, 259; 45 shortwave) (1998)

Phones 365.6 million (also 634 million cell phones)

Internet Users 253 million (2008)

*Source: CIA–*The World Factbook*

B.C.

600,000–400,000	First hominids—Lantian Man and Peking Man
80,000	Appearance of modern man, *Homo sapiens*, in China
7,000	Beginnings of agriculture and of Neolithic period
5,000	Yangshao culture
	Longshan culture
2205–1765	Xia—earliest recorded dynasty
1523–1027	Shang Dynasty flourishes in Huang He (Yellow River) Valley
1027–771	Western Zhou Dynasty
	First mathematical textbooks
	"Mandate from Heaven" concept originated
770–256	Eastern Zhou
	Spring and Autumn Period (722–476)
	Confucius (551–479)
	Laozi, founder of Taoism (570–490)
	Warring States period (475–221)
221–206	Qin Dynasty
	First emperor unites China
	First Great Wall completed
	Terracotta army statues built to guard imperial tomb at Xian
206 B.C.–A.D. 220	Han Dynasty
	Confucianism accepted as state ideology
	Western Han (206 B.C.– A.D. 24)
	Eastern Han (A.D. 24–220)
	Buddhism enters China
	Technology of papermaking developed
	Seismograph invented

A.D.

220–581	Disunity and partition
	Known as "three kingdoms and six dynasties"
	Chinese economic center shifts south to Chang Jiang (Yangtze River)
581–618	Sui Dynasty
	Grand Canal built from Hangzhou to Beijing
	Great Wall partially rebuilt
618–907	Tang Dynasty
	China's Golden Age; arts and literature flourish

907–960	Five Dynasties and Ten Kingdoms
	Invasion of nomadic tribes
1023	Chinese are first to use paper currency
960–1279	Song Dynasty
	Northern Song Dynasty (960–1127)
	Southern Song Dynasty (1127–1279)
	Marco Polo in China (1271–1292)
1279–1368	Yuan Dynasty (Mongol rule)
	Kublai Khan (1214–1294)
1368–1644	Ming Dynasty
	Sea voyages to South China Sea, the Indian Ocean, and east Africa
	First Dalai Lama (1447) in Tibet
	Arrival of Western traders
1644–1911	Qing Dynasty (Manchu rule)
	Opium Wars (1839–1842)
	Hong Kong ceded to Great Britain (1842)
	Taiping Rebellion (1850–1864)
	Boxer Uprising (1900)
1877	Former U.S. President Ulysses S. Grant visits China
1899	Future U.S. President Herbert Hoover works in China as a mining engineer
1911	End of 2,000 years of imperial rule in China
	Sun Yat-sen proclaimed president of the Republic of China
1921	Communist Party founded in Shanghai
1926	Chiang Kai-shek becomes Nationalist leader after Sun Yat-sen dies
1927	Nationalists purge Communists
1931	Japan seizes Manchuria
1934–1935	Mao Zedong and followers retreat to northwest China on Long March
1937	Japan invades China
	Nationalists and Communists form United Front
1937–1945	China and Japan at war
1941	Japan bombs Pearl Harbor; United States becomes ally of China
	U.S. volunteer fliers form "Flying Tigers" in air bases in China outside of Japanese occupation
1945	Japan surrenders

121

1946–1949	Civil war ends as the Communist People's Liberation Army defeats Nationalist forces
1949	Chiang Kai-shek and Nationalists flee to Taiwan, and Mao Zedong proclaims People's Republic of China
1950	Korean War begins; China sends troops into Korea
1951	China sends army units to Tibet
1953	Korean War ends in a truce
1956–1957	"Hundred Flowers" campaign; critics of government are later punished
1958	"Great Leap Forward" campaign and People's Communes established; widespread famine
1959	Tibetan uprising brings harsh reprisals from Beijing Dalai Lama flees to India
1960	Rift between China and Soviet Union
1962	China in border war with India
1964	China explodes first nuclear bomb; 31 more bombs follow over the years
1966–1976	Cultural Revolution
1969	Chinese clash with Soviet troops at Ussuri River border in northeast Manchuria
1971	People's Republic of China replaces Taiwan at the United Nations
1972	Richard Nixon becomes the first sitting U.S. president to visit China
1975	Chiang Kai-shek dies U.S. President Gerald Ford visits China
1976	Mao Zedong dies
1977	Deng Xiaoping takes charge in China, initiates program of economic changes, including early encouragement of Western investment in China
1979	United States recognizes People's Republic of China Deng visits United States 16-day border war between China and Vietnam
1981	Special Economic Zones created along east coast
1984	U.S. President Ronald Reagan visits China
1989	Brutal suppression of democracy movement in Tiananmen Square in Beijing Jiang Zemin chosen as party secretary-general U.S. President George H.W. Bush visits China
1990	Asian Games are held in Beijing

1997	Deng Xiaoping dies
	Hong Kong returns to Chinese rule
	Chinese President Jiang Zemin visits United States
1998	U.S. President Bill Clinton visits China
1999	Portugal returns Macau to China
2001	China joins World Trade Organization
	The 2008 Summer Olympics awarded to Beijing
	U.S. President George W. Bush visits Shanghai for Asia Pacific Economic Conference
2002	U.S. President George W. Bush makes first official visit to China
2003	Hu Jintao becomes party general-secretary, replacing Jiang Zemin, and later becomes president
	Outbreak of SARS originated in Guangdong Province
	Three Gorges Dam sluice gates close to allow reservoir to fill up
	First Chinese taikonaut (astronaut), Lt. Col. Yang Liwei, orbits Earth 14 times in 21 hours
	Wen Jiabao is named prime minister
2004	Jiang Zemin steps down as chairman of the Military Commission
2006	President Hu Jintao visited the United States, focusing on economic common ground rather than political differences between the two countries
	For the first time, China exported more cars than it imported
2008	Hu Jintao was re-elected president in March
	May 12 earthquake in Sichuan Province kills 80,000, deflecting China's preparations for the Olympics
	In September three astronauts were launched on a Shenzhen 7 rocket; the first Chinese space walk was part of this flight
2009	Shanghai prepares to host Expo 2010, a world's fair expected to bring in some 70 million visitors over a six-month period
	Hu Jintao and Wen Jiabao continue in their posts

Bibliography

Avedon, John F. *In Exile from the Land of Snows*. New York: Alfred A. Knopf, 1984.

Benewick, Robert, and Stephanie Donald. *The State of China Atlas: Mapping the World's Fastest-Growing Economy*. New York: Penguin, 1999.

Cannon, Terry, and Alan Jenkins, eds. *The Geography of Contemporary China: The Impact of Deng Xiaoping's Decade*. New York: Routledge, 1990.

Cotterell, Arthur. *China: A Cultural History*. New York: Penguin, 1988.

Dreyer, June Teufel. *China's Political System: Modernization and Tradition, 3rd ed*. London: Longman, 2000.

Economy, Elizabeth C. *The River Runs Black: The Environmental Challenge to China's Future*. Ithaca, New York: Cornell University Press, 2004.

Fairbank, John K., and Merle Goldman. *China: A New History*. Cambridge: Belknap Press, 1999.

Hessler, Peter. *Oracle Bones*. New York. HarperCollins. 2006.

_____. *River Town*. New York. HarperCollins, 2001.

Ho, Yong. *China. An Illustrated History*. New York: Hippocrene Books, Inc., 2000.

Hook, Brian, ed. *The Cambridge Encyclopedia of China, 2nd Rev. ed*. New York: Cambridge University Press, 1994.

Hunter, Alan, and John Sexton. *Contemporary China*. New York: St. Martin's Press, 1999.

Lardy, Nicholas R. *Agriculture in China's Modern Economic Development*. Cambridge: Cambridge University Press, 1983.

Leeming, F. *The Changing Geography of China*. Oxford: Blackwell, 1993.

Mackerras, Colin and Yorke, Amanda. *The Cambridge Handbook of Contemporary China*. Cambridge: Cambridge University Press, 1991.

Menzies, Gavin. *1421*. London: Bantam Books, 2003.

Mones, Nicole. *Lost in Translation*. New York. Delta/Random House. 1998.

_____. *The Last Chinese Chef*. Boston. Houghton Mifflin. 2007.

Ryder, Grainne. *Damming the Three Gorges: What Dam-Builders Don't Want You to Know*. Toronto: Probe International, 1990.

Salisbury, Harrison E. *The Long March: The Untold Story*. New York: Harper and Row, 1985.

Shambaugh, D., ed. *Greater China: The Next Superpower?* Oxford: Oxford University Press, 1995.

Spence, Jonathan D. *The Chan's Great Continent: China in Western Minds.* New York: W.W. Norton, 1998.

Troost, J. Maartin. *Lost on Planet China.* New York: Broadway Books, 2008.

Tsai, Jung-fang. *Hong Kong in Chinese History.* New York: Columbia University Press, 1993.

Winchester, Simon. *The River at the Centre of the World: A Journey Up the Yangtze and Back in Chinese Time.* London: Viking, 1997.

Wong, Jan. *Red China Blues: From Mao to Now.* New York: Doubleday and Co., 1999.

Zhao, Songqiao. *Geography of China: Environment, Resources, Population and Development.* New York: Wiley, 1994.

Further Reading

Chang, Lesley. *Factory Girls: From Village to City in a Changing China.* New York: Spiegel & Grau, Random House Publishing Group, 2008.

Ebrey, Patricia Buckley and Kwang-ching Liu. *The Cambridge Illustrated History of China.* New York: Cambridge University Press, 1999.

Fenby, Jonathan. *Modern China: The Rise and Fall of a Great Power, 1850 to the Present.* New York: Ecco, 2008.

Fisher, Leonard Everett. *Great Wall of China.* Madison, Wis: Turtleback Books, 1999.

Gascoigne, Bamber. *The Dynasties of China: A History.* Philadelphia: Running Press, 2003.

Kalman, Bobbie. *China the Land.* San Val, 2001.

Malaspina, Ann. *The Chinese Revolution and Mao Zedong in World History.* New York: Enslow Publishers, 2004.

Web sites

Chinese Embassy in Washington
  http://www.china-embassy.org
  Embassy of the People's Republic of China in the United States of America.

Creaders Net News
  http://www.creadersnet.com/
  News about Chinese culture, business, travel.

History for Kids: China
  http://www.historyforkids.org/learn/china/index.htm
  Information about the culture, history, economy, religion, art history, etc.

Kids Past: China
  http://www.kidspast.com/world-history/0125-civilization-in-china.php
  A free children's learning network.

Index

Index

Author **GARY T. WHITEFORD**, a Canadian, earned degrees in geography, a B.A. from York University in Toronto, an M.A. from Clark University, and a Ph.D. from the University of Oklahoma. He has been teaching geography in the Faculty of Education at the University of New Brunswick since 1974. He has presented over 20 papers at various conferences over the years, authored numerous journal articles, and co-edited an acclaimed atlas of the world. The author has lived in Japan and travelled extensively in China and parts of Southeast Asia. Dr. Whiteford is an active member of the National Council for Geographic Education and the Canadian Association of Geographers.

Author **CHRISTOPHER L. SALTER** is professor and chair emeritus of the geography department at the University of Missouri-Columbia. He spent three years teaching English and economic geography at Tunghai University in Taiwan and has traveled to East Asia eight times. He is the author of more than 120 articles and more than a dozen books, including South Korea, North Korea, and Taiwan in Chelsea House's MODERN WORLD NATIONS series.

Series editor **CHARLES F. GRITZNER** is Distinguished Professor of Geography Emeritus at South Dakota State University. He retired after 50 years of college teaching and now looks forward to what he hopes to be many more years of research and writing. Gritzner has served as both president and executive director of the National Council for Geographic Education and has received the council's highest honor, the George J. Miller Award for Distinguished Service to Geographic Education, as well as other honors from the NCGE, the Association of American Geographers, and other organizations.